MARCO

ITALIAN

* Italian = official language

> Words are wonderful – they let us connect with each other, experience new worlds, and live life to the full.

In this book, we've collected together all the key terms and phrases you'll need so that you'll never be lost for words during your adventures in a foreign culture and with a foreign language.

With our cheat sheet, you'll always be ready to deal with any linguistic surprises that come your way.

And if you're still stuck for words, our 'point & show' pictures are an easy way to keep on communicating.

Have a wonderful trip!

How much is it?

Quanto costa?

[kwanto kosta]

> PRONUNCIATION MADE EASY

Don't be shy, just get stuck in: our simple phonetic pronunciation guides will help you pronounce all the words, terms and phrases in this book easily and correctly.

> 'POINT & SHOW' PICTURES

A picture is worth a thousand words. Whether you're out shopping, in a restaurant, at a hotel or need help with your car, our 'point & show' pictures will help you on your way.

> INSTANT INFORMATION

FROM A TO Z
All the key themes in alphabetical order: from Doctor's visits to telephone conversations.

DICTIONARY
An A to Z of the most important words. How handy!

CONTENTS

> MENUS

Order with ease and tuck in with pleasure – foreign language menus will never be an indecipherable mystery again.

> A PACKED SCHEDULE

Do you want culture, adventure, theatre, diving trips, or language and cooking classes? We've got phrases to make your trip even more exciting.

> LOCAL KNOWLEDGE

Insider Tips To help you pass for an insider, not just a tourist.

DOS AND DON'TS!
Help you to avoid faux pas.

WARNING! SLANG
Understand the locals better!

The colours, patterns and materials below are handy for shopping trips.
You'll find more help for (almost!) every situation throughout this book.

PRONUNCIATION

To make life easier, we've included a simple pronunciation guide after all the Italian words and phrases in this book. Just pronounce most of the sounds exactly as you would if you were reading them in English.

There are a few concepts in Italian pronunciation that will be new to English speakers. Bear the following notes in mind as you go along and you'll be sounding like a local in no time:

double consonants – Italian words are are full of double consonants (e.g. pizza, casso, nonno). These should be stressed and exaggerated. To do this, say the first letter, pause for a beat, then carry on with the second (think: pizza = peet...sa). We've added a dot (') between the double letters in the pronunciation guide to show you exactly where to place this pause (e.g. pizza = peet'sa).

roll all your 'r's – and really go to town when you see a double **'rr'** (e.g. burro, arrivo)!

stress – Italian words are usually stressed on the second-to-last syllable (e.g. ristorante = rees-tor-AN-teh). Whenever this isn't the case, we've added a dot under the corresponding vowel to show you where to stress the word (e.g. piccolo, giovane).

the vowels 'e' and 'o' – 'e' should sound like the **'ai'** in the English word 'fair', while the **'o'** should be pronounced like the **'oa'** in 'board'.

ow – in this book, pronounce this sound as it appears in the English words "how" and "now" (and not "below").

hyphens – hyphens have been used to make the pronunciation guide easier to read. All the sounds connected by hyphens should be joined together when you say them out loud.

MASCULINE OR FEMININE?

Italian words come in two genders: masculine and feminine. It's usually very easy to tell them apart. If you see a word ending in ~a, it's more than likely to be feminine (e.g. la casa = the house), while most words ending in ~o are masculine (e.g. il treno = the train).

Any exceptions to this rule have been marked out in this book, as have the genders of any words that end in other letters. We've done this in two ways: 1) by placing an m or an f after the words in the text (e.g. mano f = hand), and 2) by including the appropriate Italian word for *the* in front of the noun in question (e.g. **il** sole = the sun).

The can be written several ways in Italian. That might sound daunting, but it's actually a very handy way of finding out the genders of words. Just keep the following rules in mind: Masculine singular words are preceded by: *il* and *lo*. Masculine plural words are accompanied by: *i* and *gli*. Feminine singular words are preceded by: *la*. Finally, feminine plural words are accompanied by: *le*.

ABBREVIATIONS

adj	adjective (aggettivo)		pl	plural (plurale)
adv	adverb (avverbio)		qc	qualcosa (something)
sth	something (qualcosa)		qlc	qualcuno (someone)
m	masculine (maschile)		s.o.	someone (qualcuno)
f	feminine (femminile)			

> ## SEA VIEWS AND EXTRA BEDS

Whether you want a dreamy seaside hotel or an extra bed in your room: arrange it all by email, by fax or over the phone and you can go on holiday relaxed in the knowledge that everything's sorted out.

BOOKING BY EMAIL

HOTEL | ALBERGO [albairgo]

Dear Sir/Madam,
I would like to reserve a (single/double/twin) bedroom for (two) nights from the 28th to the 30th of June. I would be grateful if you could send me confirmation of this reservation and let me know the price for the two nights including breakfast. Many thanks in advance. Best wishes,

PLANNING YOUR TRIP

Vorrei prenotare una camera singola/matrimoniale/doppia per (due) notti dal (28) al (30) giugno. Vi prego di informarmi sulle Vs. disponibilità e sulle tariffe per il pernottamento (e la mezza pensione).
Distinti saluti.

■ RENTAL CARS | MACCHINA A NOLEGGIO [mak'keena a nolej'jo] ■

Dear Sir/Madam,
I would like to rent a small car/midrange car/(7-seater) minivan from Florence airport from the 20th to the 27th of July. I would like to return the car to Milan Linate Airport, as my

return flight leaves from there. Could you please send me your prices and let me know which documents I will require?
Best wishes,

Vorrei noleggiare un'automobile di piccola (un'utilitaria)/media/un minibus (a 7 posti) dal 20 al 27 luglio all'aeroporto di Firenze e restituirla all'aeroporto di Linate/Milano dal quale ripartirò. Vi prego di mandarmi informazioni sulle tariffe e sui documenti necessari.
Distinti saluti.

ACCOMMODATION ENQUIRIES

I'm looking for a nice hotel/bed and breakfast (with good food) in the old town.	Cerco un bell'albergo/bed and breakfast nel centro storico (con cucina particolarmente buona). [chairko oon bel'lalbairgo/bed and brekfast nel chentro storeeko (kon koocheena parteekolarmenteh bwona)]
Is it central/quiet/ near the beach?	Si trova in centro/in una posizione tranquilla/ vicino al mare? [see trova een chentro/een oona pozeet-syoneh trankweel'la/veecheeno al mareh]
How much does it cost per week?	Quanto costa alla settimana? [kwanto kosta al'la set'teemana]
Does this accommodation have a website or an email address?	Questo alloggio ha un sito internet o un indirizzo e-mail? [kwesto al'loj'jo a oon seeto eentairnet o oon eendeereet'so ee-mayl]

hotel	albergo [albairgo]
guest house	pensione f [pen-syoneh]
room in a family home	sistemazione f in famiglia [seestemat-syoneh een fameel-ya]
(holiday/vacation) accommodation	appartamento (per le vacanze) [ap'partamento (pair leh vakant-seh)]

HOTEL/GUEST HOUSE/ROOMS
ALBERGO/PENSIONE/CAMERE [albairgo/pen-syoneh/kamair-eh]

 Where to Stay: page 68

I'd like to stay in a hotel, but nothing too expensive – something mid-priced.	Cerco un albergo, ma non troppo caro, a prezzo moderato. [chairko oon albairgo, ma non trop'po karo, a pret'so modairato]

I'm looking for a hotel with...	Cerco un albergo con ... [chairko oon albairgo kon]
a swimming pool.	piscina. [peesheena]
a golf course.	campo da golf. [kampo da golf]
tennis courts.	campi m, pl da tennis. [kampee da ten'nees]
Can you give me a...	Potrebbe darmi una ... [potreb'beh darmee oona]
...quiet room	... camera tranquilla? [kamaira trankweel'la]
...room with a view?	... camera con vista? [kamaira kon veesta]
...room with a balcony?	... camera con balcone? [kamaira kon balkoneh]
Is it possible to put an extra bed in the room?	Potrebbe aggiungere un altro letto in una delle camere? [potreb'beh aj'joonjaireh oon altro let'to een oona del'leh kamaireh]

HOLIDAY HOMES/HOLIDAY APARTMENTS
CASE/APPARTAMENTI PER VACANZE [kaseh/ap'partamentee pair vakant-seh]

> Where to Stay: page 74

I'm looking for a self-catering flat or holiday chalet.	Cerco un appartamento o un bungalow per le vacanze. [chairko oon ap'partamento o oon boon-galow pair leh vakant-seh]
Is there...?	C'è ...? [cheh]
a kitchen	una cucina [oona koocheena]
a dishwasher	una lavastoviglie [oona lavastoveel-yeh]
a refrigerator	un frigorifero [oon freegoreefairo]
a washing machine	una lavatrice [oona lavatreecheh]
a TV	una televisione [oona televeez-yoneh]
Wi-Fi	Wi-Fi m [waee-faee]
Is electricity included in the price?	La corrente è inclusa? [la kor'renteh eh eenklooza]
Are bed linen and towels provided?	Ci sono la biancheria e gli asciugamani? [chee sono la byankairee-ya eh l-yee ashoogamaneh]
How much deposit do you require and when does it have to be paid?	Quant'è la caparra e quando va pagata? [kwanteh la kapar'ra eh kwando va pagata]
Where and when should I pick up the keys?	Dove e quando posso ritirare le chiavi? [doveh eh kwando pos'so reeteerareh leh kyavee]

CAMPING | CAMPEGGIO [kampej'jo]

I'm looking for a campsite (on the waterfront).	Cerco un bel campeggio (vicino all'acqua). [chairko oon bel'kampej'jo (veecheeno al'lak'kwa]
Is there anything you can recommend?	Potrebbe raccomandarmi qualcosa? [potreb'beh rak'komandarmee kwalkosa]

> EXPERIENCE MORE

Don't be shy! Whether it's small talk in a café, chatting away
on a shopping trip or flirting in a club – just get stuck in!
It's easier than you think and a great way to spice up your trip!

■ SAYING HELLO | SALUTARSI [salootarsee] ■

Good morning/ Good afternoon!	Buon giorno! [bwon jorno]
Good evening!	Buonasera! [bwona-saira]
Hello!/Hi!	Ciao! [chow]
How are you?	Come stai? [komeh staee]
And you?	E Lei? [eh lay], E tu? [eh too]

BASIC CONVERSATION

What's your name? Come si chiama? [komeh see kyama]/
Come ti chiami? [komeh tee kyamee]

Nice to meet you! Sono lieto/a m/f di conoscerla!
[sono l-yeto/a dee konoshairla]

May I introduce you? Le posso presentare … [leh pos'so prezentareh]
  This is...
  Ms X/Mr X. la signora X./il signor X. [la seen-yora x/eel seen-yor x]
  my partner. il mio/la mia partner m/f. [eel mee-yo/la mee-ya partnair]

■GOODBYE/BYE! | ARRIVEDERCI! [ar'reevedairchee]

Bye!	Ciao [chow]
See you later!	A più tardi! [a pyoo tardee]
See you tomorrow!	A domani! [a domanee]
See you soon!	A presto! [a presto]
Good night!	Buona notte! [bwona not'teh]
It was nice to meet you.	Che bello aver La/ti conosciuto/a m/f.
	[keh bel'lo avair la/tee konoshooto/a]

■PLEASE | PER FAVORE [pair favoreh]

Could you do me a favour?	Le posso chiedere un favore? [leh pos'so kyedaireh oon favoreh]
Can you help me, please?	Mi può aiutare, per favore? [mee pwo a-yootareh, pair favoreh]
May I?	Permette? [pairmet'teh]
Don't mention it.	Prego! [prego]
You're welcome.	Non c'è di che. [non cheh dee keh]
With pleasure!	Con piacere! [kon pyachaireh]

■THANK YOU! | GRAZIE! [grat-syeh]

Thank you very much!	Tante grazie! [tanteh grat-syeh]
Yes, thank you!	Grazie, molto volentieri! [grat-syeh, molto volent-yairee]
No, thank you!	No, grazie! [no, grat-syeh]
Thank you. The same to you!	Grazie, altrettanto! [grat-syeh, altret'tanto]
That's very kind of you, thank you!	Molto gentile, grazie! [molto jenteeleh, grat-syeh]

■I'M SORRY! | SCUSI! [skoozee]

I'm sorry (I'm late)!	Mi dispiace (per il ritardo)!
	[mee deespyacheh (pair eel reetardo)]
What a pity!	Peccato! [pek'kato]

■ALL THE BEST! | TANTE BELLE COSE! [tanteh bel'leh koseh]

Congratulations!	Auguri! [owgooree]
Happy birthday!	Tanti auguri per il compleanno!
	[tantee owgooree pair eel kompleh-an'no]
Good luck!	Buona fortuna! [bwona fortoona]

BASIC CONVERSATION

COMPLIMENTS | COMPLIMENTI [kompleementee]

How nice/lovely!	Che bello! [keh bel'lo]
That's wonderful/great!	È meraviglioso! [eh mairaveel-yoso]
You speak very good English.	Lei lo parla molto bene l'inglese. [lay lo parla molto beneh leen-gleseh]
You're looking well!	La vedo bene. [la vedo beneh]
I think you're very nice.	La trovo molto simpatico/a m/f. [la trovo molto seempateeko/a]

LOCAL KNOWLEDGE

Insider Tips

"Buonasera!"

In Tuscany, the locals start saying *buonasera* [bwona-saira] ("good evening") as early as 2pm – just after lunch. The rest of Italy wait until about 4–5pm.

Forms of Address

It's normal in Italy to call people by their title or the name of their job: e.g. *Ingegnere* [eenjen-yaireh] ("Engineer"). You can also refer to people using both their job title and their surname (*Ingegnere X* = Mr X) but it sounds much more formal and aloof.

Greetings

When you meet someone you don't know very well, or in a formal context, greet them with *buongiorno* [bwon-joorno] ("good morning/day") or *buonasera* [bwona-saira] ("good evening"). When you get to know them better, use *Ciao!* [chow] or *Ciao, come va?* [chow, komeh va] ("Hi! How's it going?"). Italians also kiss good friends on the cheeks (left cheek first, then right), but men will only kiss other men they know very well indeed. Say goodbye to your friends with *Ci vediamo!* [chee ved-yamo] ("We'll see each other!").

"Permesso"

Visitors in Italy say *permesso* [pairmes'so] ("permission") before setting foot in someone's house (after being invited in by the host, of course!).

Compliments to the Chef

When eating in Italy, don't hesitate to compliment your food extravagantly. Eating in rapt silence can be interpreted as disappointment, so the better the food, the louder and more detailed your praise should be. Here are a few compliments to get you started: *che buono!* [keh bwono] ("very tasty!"); *buonissimo!* [bwonees'seemo] ("very good!"); *ottimo!* [ot'teemo] ("magnificent!"); *eccellente!* [et'chelenteh] ("excellent!"); *che delizia!* [keh deleet-sya] ("delicious!"); *squisito!* [skwee-zeeto] ("exquisite"); and *eccezionale!* [et'chet-syonaleh] ("exceptional").

beautiful	bello [bel'to]
excellent	ottimo [ot'teemo]
friendly	gentile [jenteeleh], cortese [kortezeh]
impressive	impressionante [eempres'syonanteh]
nice	simpatico [seempateeko]
pleasant	piacevole [pyachevoleh]
pretty	carino [kareeno], grazioso [grat-syoso]
tasty	squisito [skweezeeto], gustoso [goostoso]

■ SMALL TALK | CHIACCHIERE [kyak'kyaireh] ■

PERSONAL INFORMATION GENERALITÀ [jenairaleeta]

What do you do for a living?	Qual è la Sua/tua professione?
	[kwal eh la soo-a/too-a profes'syoneh]
I'm a...	Sono … [sono]
I work for...	Lavoro presso … [lavoro pres'so]
I'm still at school.	Vado ancora a scuola. [vado ankora a skwola]
I'm a student.	Sono studente/essa universitario/a m/f.
	[sono stoodenteh/es'sa ooneevairseetar-yo/ya]
How old are you?	Quanti anni ha/hai? [kwantee an'nee a/aee]
I'm (twenty-four).	Ho (ventiquattro) anni. [o (venteekwat'tro) an'nee]

ORIGIN AND STAY PROVENIENZA E RESIDENZA [proveen-yent-sa eh reseedent-sa]

Where do you come from?	Di dov'è Lei?/Di dove sei tu? [dee doveh lay/dee doveh say too]
I'm from (London).	Sono di (Londra). [sono dee (londra)]
I'm from England.	Vengo d'Inghilterra. [ven-go deen-geeltair'ra]
Have you been here long?	È/Sei qui da molto? [eh/say kwee da molto]
I've been here since...	Sono qui da … [sono kwee da]
How long are you staying?	Quanto si ferma/ti fermi? [kwanto see fairma/tee fairmee]
Do you like it?	Che cosa ne pensa? [keh kosa neh pensa]
What's your e-mail address?	Qual è il tuo indirizzo email?
	[kwal eh eel too-o eendeereet'so ee-mayl]

HOBBIES HOBBY [ob'bee]

What do you do in your spare time?	Cosa fa/fai nel tempo libero?
	[kosa fa/faee nel tempo leebairo]
I'm interested in	Mi interesso di … [mee eentaires'so dee]
art/culture/	l'arte f/la cultura [larteh/la kooltoora]
architecture/fashion.	l'architettura/la moda [larkeetet'toora/la moda]
Are you on Facebook?	È/Sei su Facebook? [eh/say soo fays-book]
cards, board games	giochi m, pl a carte [jokee a karteh]/da tavola [da tavola]
cinema, movies	cinema/film m [cheenema/feelm]

BASIC CONVERSATION

computer games	videogiochi m, pl [veedayoh-jokee]
cooking	cucinare [koocheenareh]
learning languages	studiare lingue f, pl [stood-yareh leen-gweh]
listening to music	ascoltare musica [askoltareh moozeeka]
making music	fare musica [fareh moozeeka]
meeting friends	incontrare amici m, pl [eenkontrareh ameechee]
painting	dipingere [deepeenjaireh]
reading	leggere [lej'jaireh]
taking photos	fotografare [fotografareh]
travelling	viaggiare [vee-yaj'jareh]

SPORT   SPORT [sport]

 A Packed Schedule: page 84

What sports do you do?	Quale sport pratica Lei? [kwaleh sport prateeka lay]
I play football/ tennis/rugby/ volleyball/table tennis.	Io gioco a [ee-yo joko a] … calcio [kalchyo]/ tennis m [ten'nees]/pallavolo [pal'lavolo]/ pallamano [pal'lamano]/ping-pong. [peeng-pong]
I go to the gym/to yoga regularly.	Vado in palestra/faccio yoga regolarmente. [vado een palestra/fat'chyo yoga regolarmenteh]
I go jogging/swimming/ cycling.	Faccio jogging. [fat'chyo jog'geeng]/Nuoto. [nwoto]/ Vado in bicicletta. [vado een beecheeklet'ta]

MAKING A DATE | APPUNTAMENTO/FLIRT [ap'poontamento/fleert]

Have you got any plans for tomorrow?	Ha/Hai già un programma per domani? [a/aee ja oon program'ma pair domanee]
Shall we meet up this evening?	Ci vediamo stasera? [chee ved-yamo stasaira]
When shall we meet?	A che ora ci incontriamo? [a keh ora chee eenkontree-yamo]
Can I take you home?	La/Ti posso accompagnare a casa? [la/tee pos'so ak'kompan-yareh a kasa]
Have you got a boyfriend/ a girlfriend?	Hai un ragazzo [aee oon ragat'so]/ una ragazza? [oona ragat'sa]
Are you married?	È sposato m/f/sposata m/f? [eh spozato/spozata]
I've been looking forward to seeing you all day.	L'ho aspettata/Ti ho aspettato tutto il giorno con impazienza. [lo aspet'tata/tee o aspet'tato toot'to eel jorno kon eempat-syent-sa]
You've got beautiful eyes!	Hai degli occhi stupendi! [aee del-yee ok'kee stoopendee]
I've fallen in love with you.	Mi sono innamorato/a m/f di te! [mee sono een'namorato/a dee teh]
I love you!	Ti amo! [tee amo]
I love you, too.	Io pure ti amo. [ee-yo pooreh tee amo]
I would like to sleep with you.	Vorrei andare a letto con te. [vor'ray andareh a let'to kon teh]

But only if we use a condom!	Però solo con preservativo! [pairo solo kon presairvateevo]
Do you have any condoms?	Ne hai preservativi? [neh aee presairvateevee]
Where can I buy some?	Dove posso comprarli? [doveh pos'so komprarlee]
I don't want to.	Non ne ho voglia. [non neh o vol-ya]
Please leave now!	Per favore, adesso vattene! [pair favoreh, ades'so vat'teneh]
Stop immediately!	Smettila! [zmet'teela]
Go away! / Get lost!	Sparisci! [spareeshee]
Please leave me alone!	Mi lasci in pace, per favore! [mee lashee een pacheh, pair favoreh]

TIME

TIME | L'ORA [lora]

WHAT TIME IS IT? CHE ORE SONO? [keh oreh sono]

> Time: Inside front cover

WHAT TIME?/WHEN? A CHE ORA?/QUANDO? [a keh ora/kwando]

At (eight) o'clock.	Alle (otto). [al'leh (ot'to)]
In an hour's time.	Fra un'ora. [fra oon-ora]
Between (three) and (four).	Tra le (tre) e le (quattro). [tra leh (treh) eh leh (kwat'tro)]

HOW LONG? PER QUANTO TEMPO? [pair kwanto tempo]

Two hours.	Per due ore. [pair doo-eh oreh]
From (ten) to (eleven).	Dalle (dieci) alle (undici). [dal'leh (dee-yechee) al'leh (oondeechee)]
Till (five) o'clock.	Fino alle (cinque). [feeno al'leh (cheenkweh)]

LOCAL KNOWLEDGE

Inside Tip

Just Friends?

Amico m [ameeko] and amica f [ameeka] are the words Italians use to refer to their perfectly platonic, everyday friends – e.g. that's my friend Giuseppe! – Questo è il mio amico Giuseppe! [kwesto eh eel mee-yo ameeko joosep'peh]. If your relationship is somewhat more romantic, you'll need some new vocabulary: younger people use ragazzo m [regat'so]/ragazza f [regat'sa], while people from about 40 years of age call that special someone their compagno m [kompan-yo]/compagna f [kompan-ya].

BASIC CONVERSATION

SINCE WHEN?   DA QUANDO? [da kwando]

Since (eight am).	Fin dalle (otto) del mattino. [feen dal'leh (ot'to) del mat'teeno]
For half an hour.	Da mezz'ora. [da met'sora]

OTHER EXPRESSIONS OF TIME
ULTERIORI INDICAZIONI DELL'ORA [ooltair-yoree eendeekat-syonee del'lora]

in the morning	la mattina (presto) [la mat'teena (presto)]
during the morning	la mattina [la mat'teena]
at lunchtime	a mezzogiorno [a met'sojorno]
in the afternoon	il pomeriggio [eel pomaireej'jo]
in the evening	di sera [dee saira]
at night	di notte f [dee not'teh]
the day before yesterday	l'altro ieri [laltro ee-yairee]
yesterday	ieri [ee-yairee]
ten minutes ago	dieci minuti fa [dee-yechee meenootee fa]
today	oggi [oj'jee]
now	ora [ora]
tomorrow	domani [domanee]
the day after tomorrow	dopo domani [dopo domanee]
this week	questa settimana [kwesta set'teemana]
at the weekend	a fine f settimana [a feeneh set'teemana]
on Sunday	domenica [domeneeka]
in a fortnight's time	fra quindici giorni [fra kweendeechee jornee]
next year	l'anno prossimo [lan'no pros'seemo]
sometimes	a volte [a volteh]
every half hour	ogni mezz'ora [on-yee met'sora]
every hour	ogni ora [on-yee ora]
every day	tutti i giorni m, pl [toot'tee ee jornee], giornaliero [jornal-yairo]
every other day	ogni due giorni [on-yee doo-eh jornee]
within a week	entro una settimana [entro oona set'teemana]
soon	presto [presto]

THE DATE | DATA [data]

What's the date today?	Quanti ne abbiamo oggi? [kwantee neh ab'byamo oj'jee]
Today's the first of May.	Oggi è il primo maggio. [oj'jee eh eel preemo maj'jo]

DAYS OF THE WEEK | I GIORNI DELLA SETTIMANA [ee jornee del'la set'teemana]

Monday	lunedì [loonedee]
Tuesday	martedì [martedee]
Wednesday	mercoledì [mairkoledee]
Thursday	giovedì [jovedee]
Friday	venerdì [venairdee]
Saturday	sabato [sabato]
Sunday	domenica [domeneeka]

MONTHS OF THE YEAR | I MESI [ee mesee]

January	gennaio [jen'na-yo]
February	febbraio [feb'bra-yo]
March	marzo [mart-so]
April	aprile [apreeleh]
May	maggio [maj'jo]
June	giugno [joon-yo]
July	luglio [lool-yo]
August	agosto [agosto]
September	settembre [set'tembreh]
October	ottobre [ot'tobreh]
November	novembre [novembreh]
December	dicembre [deechembreh]

SEASONS | LE STAGIONI [leh stajonee]

spring	primavera [preemavaira]
summer	estate [estateh]
autumn/fall	autunno [owtoon'no]
winter	inverno [eenvairno]

HOLIDAYS | GIORNI FESTIVI [jornee festeevee]

New Year's Day	Capodanno [kapodan'no]
Good Friday	Venerdì Santo [venairdee santo]
Easter	Pasqua [paskwa]
Easter Monday	Lunedì dell'Angelo [loonedee del'lanjelo]
Liberation Day (25th of April)	Anniversario della Liberazione [an'neevairsar-yo del'la leebairat-syoneh]
Labour Day (1st of May)	Festa del lavoro [festa del lavoro]

BASIC CONVERSATION

Ascension	Assunzione [as'soont-syoneh]
Pentecost	Pentecoste [pentekosteh]
The Feast of Corpus Christi	Corpus Domini [korpoos domeenee]
Day of the Republic (National Holiday – 2nd of June)	Festa della Repubblica [festa del'la repoob'bleeka]
Assumption Day	Ferragosto [fair'ragosto]
All Saints' Day (1st of Nov)	Ognissanti [on-yees'santee], Tutti i Santi [toot'tee ee santee]
The Feast of the Immaculate Conception (8th of Dec)	Immacolata Concezione [eem'makolata konchet-syoneh]
Christmas Eve/Day	Vigilia di Natale [veejeel-ya dee nataleh]/Natale [nataleh]
New Year's Eve	notte f di San Silvestro [not'teh dee san seelvestro]

THE WEATHER

What's the weather going to be like today?	Che tempo farà oggi? [keh tempo fara oj'jee]
It's going to stay fine/ remain poor.	Rimane bello/brutto. [reemaneh bel'lo/broot'to]
It's going to get warmer/ colder.	Si sta facendo più caldo/freddo. [see sta fachendo pyoo kaldo/fred'do]
It's going to rain/snow.	Pioverà/Nevicherà. [pyovaira/neveekaira]
It's cold/hot/close.	Fa freddo/caldo./C'è afa. [fa fred'do/kaldo/cheh afa]
What's the temperature today?	Quanti gradi abbiamo oggi? [kwantee gradee ab'byamo oj'jee]
It's (20) degrees.	Abbiamo una temperatura di (venti) gradi. [ab'byamo oona tempairatoora dee (ventee) gradee]

changeable	variabile [var-yabeeleh]
cloudy	nuvoloso [noovoloso]
cold	freddo [fred'do]
flood	l'alluvione f [lal'loov-yoneh]
fog	nebbia f [neb'bya]
frost	gelo m [jelo]
high tide	alta marea [alta maraya]
hot	caldo [kaldo], (very hot) bollente [bol'lenteh]
low tide	bassa marea [bas'sa maraya]
rain	pioggia f [pyoj'ja]
snow	la neve [la neveh]
sun	il sole [eel soleh]
thunderstorm	temporale m [temporaleh]
warm	caldo [kaldo]
wind	vento m [vento]

> WHICH WAY TO THE...?

If you're lost, confused, or simply don't know where to go:
ask someone! This chapter will help you get back on track.

HOW DO I GET TO...?

Excuse me Sir/Madam/Miss, where's..., please?
Scusi signore/signora/signorina, dov'è … per favore?
[skoozee seen-yoreh/seen-yora/seen-yoreena, doveh … pair favoreh]

Excuse me, how do you get to...?
Senta, scusi, per andare a …?
[senta, skoozee, pair andareh a]

What's the quickest way to...?
Qual è la strada più breve per …?
[kwal eh la strada pyoo breveh pair]

How far is it to...?
Quanto ci vuole per andare a …?
[kwanto chee vwoleh pair andareh a]

OUT AND ABOUT

Go straight on.	Vada diritto. [vada deereet'to]
Turn left/right.	Vada a sinistra/a destra.
	[vada a seeneestra/a destra]
The first/second street on the left/right.	La prima/seconda strada a sinistra/a destra.
	[la preema/sekonda strada a seeneestra/a destra]
Cross...	Attraversi ... [at'travairsee]
the bridge.	il ponte. [eel ponteh]
the square.	la piazza. [la pyat'sa]
the street.	la strada. [la strada]
Then ask again.	Poi chięda un'altra volta.
	[poy kyeda oon-altra volta]

You can take...	Può prendere … [pwo prendaireh]
the bus./ the tram.	l'autobus. m [lowtoboos]/il tram. [eel tram]
the tube (the underground).	la metropolitana. [la metropoleetana]

AT THE BORDER

Have you got anything to declare?	Ha niente da dichiarare? [a nyenteh da deekyarareh]
Pull over to the right, please.	Si metta lì a destra! [see met'ta lee a destra]
Open the boot (trunk)/this case, please.	Apra, per favore, il bagagliaio/questa valigia. [apra, pair favoreh, eel bagal-ya-yo/kwesta valeeja]
Do I have to pay duty on this?	Lo/la devo sdoganare? [lo/la devo zdog-an-areh]
No, I've only got a few presents (gifts).	No, ho soltanto alcuni regali. [no, o soltanto alkoonee regalee]
Open the boot (trunk)/ this case, please.	Ouvrez votre coffre/cette valise, s.v.p. [oovray votruh kofruh/set valeez, seel voo play]

Christian/first name	il nome [eel nomeh]
customs	dogana [dogana]
date of birth	data di nascita [data dee nasheeta]
driving licence	la patente [la patenteh]
duty-free	esente da dazio doganale [ezenteh da dat-syo doganaleh]
enter (the country)	entrare (in un paese) [entrareh (een oon pa-ezeh)]
export n	l'esportazione f [lesportat-syoneh],
	l'esecuzione f [lezekoot-syoneh]
ID card	carta d'identità [karta deedenteeta]
import n	l'importazione f [leemportat-syoneh]
leave the country	partire (per l'estero) [parteereh (pair lestairo)]
liable to customs duty	soggetto a dazio doganale [soj'jet'to a dat-syo doganaleh]
maiden name	il nome da ragazza [eel nomeh da ragat'sa]
marital status	stato di famiglia [stato dee fameel-ya]
married	sposato [spozato]
nationality	nazionalità [nat-syonaleeta]
passport	passaporto [pas'saporto]
place of birth	luogo di nascita [lwogo dee nasheeta]
place of residence	domicilio [domeecheel-yo]
single	(man) celibe [cheleebeh], (woman) nubile [noobeeleh]
surname	il cognome [eel kon-yomeh]
valid	valido [valeedo]

TRAVELLING BY CAR/MOTORBIKE/BICYCLE

HOW DO I GET TO...? | PER ANDARE A ...? [pair andareh a]

How far is it?	Quanti chilòmetri sono? [kwantee keelometree sono]
Excuse me, is this the road to...?	Scusi, è questa la strada per …? [skoozee, eh kwesta la strada pair]
How do I get to the motorway/ highway to...?	Scusi, l'autostrada per …? [skoozee, lowtostrada pair]
Straight on until you get to... Then turn left/right.	Sempre diritto fino a … [sempreh deereet'to feeno a] Poi svolti a sinistra/destra. [poy zvoltee a seeneestra/destra]

FILL UP THE TANK, PLEASE
IL PIENO, PER FAVORE! [eel pye-no, pair favoreh]

Where's the nearest petrol/ gas station, please?	Dov'è la pròssima stazione di servizio, per favore? [doveh la pros'seema stat-syoneh dee sairveet-syo, pair favoreh]
95 octane/98 octane/diesel/ charging point for electric vehicles	benzina normale/super/gasòlio/la stazione di servizio per la ricàrica dei veìcoli [bend-zeena normaleh/soopair/gazol-yo/la stat-syoneh dee sairveet-syo pair la reekareeka day vay-eekolee]
Please check the oil level.	Scusi, potrebbe controllare il livello dell'olio? [skoozee, potreb'beh kontrol'lareh eel leevel'lo del'lol-yo]
Could you also check the radiator water, please?	Controlli anche l'acqua del radiatore, per favore. [kontrol'lee ankeh lak'kwa del rad-yatoreh, pair favoreh]
Where are the toilets, please?	Scusi, dov'è il bagno? [skoozee, doveh eel ban-yo]

PARKING | IL PARCHEGGIO [eel parkej'jo]

Is there a car park/ parking lot near here?	Scusi, c'è un parcheggio qui vicino? [skoozee, cheh oon parkej'jo kwee veecheeno]
Can I park my car here?	Mi potete rilasciàre qui il visto? [mee poteteh reelashareh kwee eel veesto]

■ BREAKDOWN | GUASTO [gwasto]

Could you help me
jump-start my car?

Potrebbe aiutarmi ad avviare la macchina?
[potreb'beh a-yootarmee ad av'vee-yareh la mak'keena]

Would you send a mechanic/
a breakdown truck, please?

Mi potrebbe mandare un meccanico?/un carro-attrezzi?
[mee potreb'beh mandareh oon mek'kaneeko/oon kar'ro-at'tret'see]

Could you give me some
petrol/gas, please?

Mi potrebbe dare un po' di benzina, per favore?
[mee potreb'beh dareh oon po dee bend-zeena, pair favoreh]

Could you help me change
the tyre/tire, please?

Mi potrebbe aiutare a cambiare la ruota?
[mee potreb'beh a-yootareh a kambyareh la roo-ota]

Could you give me a lift
to the nearest petrol
(gas) station?

Mi potrebbe dare un passaggio fino alla prossima
stazione di servizio? [mee potreb'beh dareh oon pas'saj'jo feeno
al'la pros'seema stat-syoneh dee sairveet-syo]

■ GARAGE | OFFICINA [of'feecheena]

The car won't start.

La macchina non parte. [la mak'keena non parteh]

Could you have a look?

Ci potrebbe dare un'occhiata, per favore?
[chee potreb'beh dareh oon-ok'kyata, pair favoreh]

The battery is flat.

La batteria è scarica. [la bat'tairee-ya eh skareeka]

There's something wrong
with the engine.

Il motore non va bene.
[eel motoreh non va beneh]

The brakes don't work.

I freni non sono a posto. [ee frenee non sono a posto]

...is/are faulty.

… è/sono difettoso/difettosi. [eh/sono deefet'toso/deefet'tosee]

I'm losing oil.

La macchina perde olio. [la mak'keena pairdeh ol-yo]

Change the sparkplugs, please. Cambi le candele, per favore. [kambee leh kandeleh, pair favoreh]

How much will it cost?

Quanto costerà? [kwanto kostaira]

LOCAL KNOWLEDGE

Inside Tip

> ### In the Driving Seat

In recent years, limited traffic zones (ZTL = zone a traffico limitato [zoneh a traf'feeko leemeetato])
have been set up in the centres of Italy's larger towns and cities. You can only drive
through these signposted areas at certain times of day or if you're armed with a pass. The
zones' boundaries are carefully monitored – if you drive where you shouldn't, a fine will
be sent winging its way to your door. Don't worry if your hotel is located within these
zones, however – simply call ahead and they'll be able to issue you with authorisation.
When parking, only choose spaces surrounded with blue lines: yellow parking spaces are
reserved for residents only.

ACCIDENTS | INCIDENTE [eencheedenteh]

Please call...	Chiami subito … [kyamee soobeeto]
an ambulance.	un'autoambulanza. [oon-owto-amboolant-sa]
the police.	la polizia. [la poleet-see-ya]
the fire-brigade.	i vigili del fuoco. [ee veejeelee del fwoko]
Are you injured?	È ferito/a m/f [eh faireeto/a]
Have you got a first-aid kit?	Ha materiale di pronto soccorso?
	[a matair-yaleh dee pronto sok'korso]
It was my fault.	È stata colpa mia. [eh stata kolpa mee-ya]
It was your fault.	È stata colpa Sua. [eh stata kolpa soo-a]
Shall we call the police,	Dobbiamo chiamare la polizia, o ci vogliamo mettere
or can we settle things	d'accordo fra noi? [dob'byamo kyamareh la poleet-see-ya,
ourselves?	o chee vol-yamo met'taireh dak'kordo fra noy]
I'd like my insurance company	Vorrei far regolare il danno dalla mia assicurazione.
to take care of the damage.	[vor'ray far regolareh eel dan'no dal'la mee-ya as'seekoorat-syoneh]
Please give me your name	Mi dia il Suo nome e indirizzo.
and address.	[mee dee-ya eel soo-o nomeh eh eendeereet'so]
Thank you very much	Grazie dell'aiuto.
for your help.	[grat-syeh del'la-yooto]

accelerator	l'acceleratore m [lat'chelairatoreh]
alcohol level	per mille [pair meel'leh]
automatic (transmission)	cambio automatico [kambyo owtomateeko]
backfire	l'accensione f a vuoto [lat'chen-syoneh a vwoto]
battery	la batteria [la bat'tairee-ya]
bell	campanello [kampanel'lo]
bend (in a road, etc.)	curva [koorva]
bicycle, bike	bicicletta [beecheeklet'ta]
brake pad	la guarnizione dei freni [la gwarneet-syoneh day frenee]
breakdown	guasto [gwasto]
breakdown service	soccorso stradale [sok'korso stradaleh]
cable	cavo [kavo]
car park (parking lot)	parcheggio [parkej'jo]
car wash	autolavaggio [owtolavaj'jo]
carburettor	il carburatore [eel karbooratoreh]
clutch	la frizione [la freet-syoneh]
coolant	acqua di raffreddamento [ak'kwa dee raf'fred'damento]
country road	strada maestra [strada ma-estra]
crash helmet	casco [kasko]
crossroads, junction	incrocio [eenkrochyo]
diversion/detour	la deviazione [la devee-yat-syoneh]
driving licence	la patente [la patenteh]
dynamo/alternator	la dinamo [la deenamo]

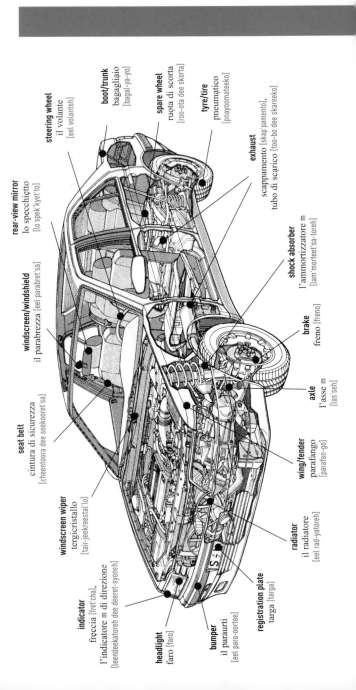

steering wheel
il volante
[eel volanteh]

boot/trunk
bagagliaio
[bagal-ya-yo]

spare wheel
ruota di scorta
[roo-ota dee skorta]

tyre/tire
pneumatico
[pnayoomateeko]

rear-view mirror
lo specchietto
[lo spek'kyet'to]

exhaust
scappamento [skap pamento],
tubo di scarico [too-bo dee skareeko]

windscreen/windshield
il parabrezza [eel parabret'sa]

shock absorber
l'ammortizzatore m
[lam morteet'sa-toreh]

seat belt
cintura di sicurezza
[cheentoora dee seekooret'sa]

brake
freno [freno]

axle
l'asse m
[las seh]

windscreen wiper
tergicristallo
[tair-jeekreestal'lo]

wing/fender
parafango
[parafan-go]

indicator
freccia [fret'cha],
l'indicatore m di direzione
[teendeekatoreh dee deeret-syoneh]

radiator
il radiatore
[eel rad-yatoreh]

headlight
faro [faro]

bumper
il paraurti
[eel para-oortee]

registration plate
targa [targa]

emergency telephone	telefono d'emergenza [telefono demairjend-za]
fan belt	cinghia [cheen-gya]
fault n	difetto [deefet'to]
fine	ammenda [am'menda], multa [moolta]
flat tyre (tire)/puncture	foratura [foratoora]
footbrake	freno a pedale [freno a pedaleh]
fuel station for electric cars	la stazione di servizio per la ricarica die veicoli [la stat-syoneh dee sairveet-syo pair la reekareeka day vaykolee]
full/high beam lights	i fari abbaglianti [ee faree ab'bal-yantee]
fully comprehensive insurance	l'assicurazione f di totale copertura [las'seekoorat-syoneh dee totaleh kopairtoora]
garage	officina [of'feecheena]
gear	marcia [marcha]
gearbox	cambio [kambyo]
green card (insurance)	carta verde [karta vairdeh]
handbrake	freno a mano [freno a mano]
hazard warning light	il lampeggiatore d'emergenza [eel lampej'jatoreh demairjend-za]
heating	riscaldamento [reeskaldamento]
hitch-hiker	l'autostoppista m/f [lowtostop'peesta]
horn	il clacson [eel klakson]
horsepower, hp	cavalli m, pl vapore, CV [kaval'lee vaporeh, chee vee]
ignition	l'accensione f [lat'chen-syoneh]
ignition key	chiavetta di accensione [kyavet'tea dee at'chen-syoneh]
ignition switch	l'interruttore m dell'accensione [leentair'root'toreh del'lat'chen-syoneh]
jack	il cric [eel kreek]
jump lead	cavo ausiliario di collegamento per la messa in moto [kavo owseel-yar-yo dee kol'legamento pair la mes'sa een moto]
lane	corsia [korsee-ya]
lorry, truck	il camion [eel kamyon]
motor, engine	il motore [eel motoreh]
motorbike	motocicletta [motocheeklet'ta]
motorway service station (rest stop)	la stazione di servizio [la stat-syoneh dee sairveet-syo], posto di ristoro [posto dee reestoro]
motorway/highway	autostrada [owtostrada]
mudguard	lamiera di protezione [lam-yaira dee protet-syoneh]
multi-storey car park/ parking lot	parcheggio a più piani [parkej'jo a pyoo pyanee], autosilo [owtoseelo]
natural gas (LPG) station	distributore m metano [deestreebootoreh metano]
octane number	numero di ottani [noomairo dee ot'tanee]
oil, oil change	olio [ol-yo], cambio dell'olio [kambyo del'lol-yo]
papers (documents)	i documenti [ee dokoomentee]
petrol/gas	benzina [bend-zeena]
petrol/gas can	lattina [lat'teena], tanica [taneeka]

petrol/gas station	stazione f di servizio [stat-syoneh dee sairveet-syo]
pump	la pompa [la pompa]
rack	il portabagagli [eel portabagal-yee]
radar speed check	controllo radar [kontrol'lo radar]
(puncture) repair kit	gli accessori m per la riparazione di forature [l-yee at'ches'soree pair la reeparat-syoneh dee foratooreh]
rim	il cerchione [eel chairkyoneh]
road map	carta automobilistica [karta owtomobeeleesteeka]
road works	il cantiere edile [eel kant-yaireh edeeleh]
scooter	il motoscooter [eel motoskootair], motoretta [motoret'ta]
screw	la vite [la veeteh]
sidelights	le luci di posizione [leh loochee dee pozeet-syoneh]
sign	targa stradale [targa stradaleh]
spanner, wrench	la chiave per dadi [la kyaveh pair dadee]
spark plug	candela [kandela]
speedometer	tachimetro [takeemetro]
starter motor	motorino d'avviamento [motoreeno dav'vee-yamento]
street, road	strada [strada], via [vee-ya]
sunroof	tetto apribile [tet'to apreebeeleh]
toll (charge)	il pedaggio [eel pedaj'jo]
tools	l'utensile m [lootenseeleh], attrezzo [at'tret'so]
tow (away)	rimorchiare [reemorkyareh], trainare [traee-nareh]
towrope	cavo da rimorchio [kavo da reemorkyo]
traffic jam	ingorgo [een-gorgo]
traffic lights	semaforo [semaforo]
valve	valvola [valvola]
warning triangle	triangolo [tree-yan-golo]

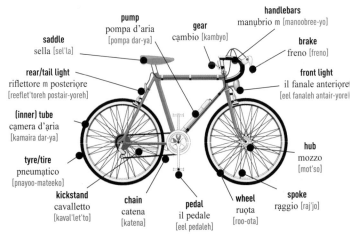

handlebars
manubrio m [manoobree-yo]

pump
pompa d'aria
[pompa dar-ya]

gear
cambio [kambyo]

brake
freno [freno]

saddle
sella [sel'la]

rear/tail light
riflettore m posteriore
[reeflet'toreh postair-yoreh]

front light
il fanale anteriore
[eel fanaleh antair-yoreh]

(inner) tube
camera d'aria
[kamaira dar-ya]

hub
mozzo
[mot'so]

tyre/tire
pneumatico
[pnayoo-mateeko]

kickstand
cavalletto
[kaval'let'to]

chain
catena
[katena]

pedal
il pedale
[eel pedaleh]

wheel
ruota
[roo-ota]

spoke
raggio [raj'jo]

OUT AND ABOUT

CAR/MOTORBIKE/BICYCLE HIRE
AUTONOLEGGIO/NOLEGGIO DI MOTOCICLI/NOLEGGIO DI BICICLETTE

I'd like to hire... for (2) days/ for (1) week.
Vorrei noleggiare … per (due) giorni/(una) settimana.
[vor'ray nolej'jareh … pair (doo-eh) jornee/(oona) set'teemana]

  a car/a camper van/
una macchina [oona mak'keena], un camper [oon kampair],

  a scooter/a bicycle
uno scooter [oono skootair], una bicicletta [oona beecheeklet'ta]

I'd like an automatic/ air-conditioning/ a navigation system.
Possibilmente con il cambio automatico/ il climatizzatore/il navigatore. [pos'seebeelmenteh kon eel kambyo owtomateeko/eel kleemateet'satoreh/eel naveegatoreh]

How much does it cost per day/week?
Qual è il forfait giornaliero/settimanale?
[kwal eh eel forfa-eet jornal-yairo/set'teemanaleh]

What do you charge per km?
Quanto si paga per ogni chilometro percorso?
[kwanto see paga pair on-yee keelometro pairkorso]

Does the vehicle have comprehensive insurance?
Il veicolo è assicurato contro tutti i rischi?
[eel vaykolo eh as'seekoorato kontro toot'tee ee reeskee]

Is it possible to return the car in/at...?
È possibile riconsegnare la macchina a …?
[eh pos'seebeeleh reekonsen-yareh la mak'keena]

TRAVELLING BY PLANE

DEPARTURE | DECOLLO [dekol'lo]

Where's the counter for (name of airline)?
Dov'è lo sportello della …?
[doveh lo sportel'lo del'la]

When's the next flight to...?
Quando c'è un aereo per …? [kwando cheh oon a-airayo pair]

I'd like to book a single/ return flight to...
Vorrei prenotare un volo di sola andata/ di andata e ritorno per …
[vor'ray prenotareh oon volo dee sola andata/dee andata eh reetorno pair]

Are there still seats available?
Ci sono ancora posti liberi?
[chee sono ankora postee leebairee]

I'd like to cancel this flight.
Vorrei annullare questo volo.
[vor'ray an'nool'lareh kwesto volo]

Can I take this on as hand luggage/baggage?
Posso portare con me il bagaglio a mano?
[pos'so portareh kon meh eel bagal-yo a mano]

Is the plane to... late?
L'aereo per … è in ritardo?
[la-airayo pair … eh een reetardo]

My luggage/baggage is missing.	Il mio bagaglio è stato smarrito. [eel mee-yo bagal-yo eh stato zmar'reeto]
My suitcase has been damaged.	La mia valigia è stata danneggiata. [la mee-ya valeeja eh stata dan'nej'jata]
airline	compagnia aerea [kompan-yee-a a-airaya]
airport bus	collegamento pullman con l'aeroporto [kol'legamento pool'lman kon la-airoporto]
airport tax	i diritti aeroportuali [ee deereet'tee a-airo-port-oo-walee]
boarding card	carta d'imbarco [karta deembarko]
booking	la prenotazione [la prenotat-syoneh]
cancel	annullare [an'nool'lareh]
change (a booking)	cambiare il biglietto [kambyareh eel beel-yet'to]
check in v	fare il check-in [fareh eel chek-een]
connection	coincidenza [ko-eencheedent-sa]
counter	sportello [sportel'lo]
delay	ritardo [reetardo]
departure	decollo [dekol'lo]
direct flight	volo diretto [volo deeret'to]
duty-free shop	spaccio porto-franco [spat'chyo porto-franko]
e-ticket	il biglietto elettronico [eel beel-yet'to elet'troneeko]
emergency exit	uscita d'emergenza [oosheeta demairjend-za]
emergency landing	atterraggio di fortuna [at'tair'raj'jo dee fortoona]
flight	volo [volo]
hand luggage/baggage	bagaglio a mano [bagal-yo a mano]
landing	atterraggio [at'tair'raj'jo]
life jacket	giubbetto di salvataggio [joob'bet'to dee salvataj'jo]
luggage/baggage	bagaglio [bagal-yo]
luggage/baggage claim	la spedizione bagagli [la spedeet-syoneh bagal-yee]
on board	a bordo [a bordo]
online booking	la prenotazione online [la prenotat-syoneh onla-een]
pilot	il/la pilota [eel/la peelota]
plane	aereo [a-airayo]
route	tratto (di volo) [trat'to (dee volo)]
scheduled time of departure	volo regolare [volo regolareh]
security control	controllo di sicurezza [kontrol'lo dee seekooret'sa]
sick bag	il sacchetto [eel sak'ket'to]
steward/stewardess	l'assistente m/f di volo [las'seestenteh dee volo]
stopover	scalo [skalo]
time of arrival	orario d'arrivo [orar-yo dar'reevo]
timetable	orario aereo [orar-yo a-airayo]
window seat	posto al finestrino [posto al feenestreeno]

TRAVELLING BY TRAIN

AT THE STATION | ALLA STAZIONE [al'la stat-syoneb]

When's the next train to...?	Quando parte il prossimo treno per ...? [kwando parteh eel pros'seemo treno pair]
A second-class/first-class single to..., please.	Un biglietto di andata, seconda/prima classe ... per favore [oon beel-yet'to dee andata, sekonda/preema klas'seh ... pair favoreh]
Two returns to..., please.	Due biglietti per ..., andata e ritorno, per favore. [doo-eh beel-yet'tee pair ..., andata eh reetorno, pair favoreh]
Is there an economy fare?	C'è una tariffa ridotta? [cheh oona tareef'fa reedot'ta]
Is there a reduction for children/students?	C'è una riduzione per bambini/per studenti? [cheh oona reedoot-syoneh pair bambeenee/pair stoodentee]
Do I have to reserve a seat?	Devo prenotare il posto? [devo prenotareh eel posto]
Is the train from... running late?	È in ritardo il treno proveniente da ...? [eh een reetardo eel treno provenyenteh da]
(Where) Do I have to change?	(Dove) Devo cambiare? [(doveh) devo kambyareh]
Which platform/track does the train for... leave from?	Da quale binario parte il treno per ...? [da kwaleh beenar-yo parteh eel treno pair]
Can I take a bycicle?	Posso portare la bicicletta? [pos'so portareh la beecheeklet'ta]

LOCAL KNOWLEDGE

Insider Tip

> ### Rail Reductions

Some hotels – particularly those on the Adriatic coast – will give you some money towards the price of your journey if you make your way there using the Italian Rail Service (Ferrovie dello Stato (FS) [fer'rovee-yeh del'lo stato]). Just ask about the scheme when you book: Concedete un rimborso parziale per le spese del biglietto del treno? [konchedeteh oon reemborso part-syaleh pair leh speseh del beel-yet'to del treno]

Excuse me, is this seat free?	Scusi, è libero questo posto? [skoozee, eh leebairo kwesto posto]
Does this train stop in...?	Questo treno si ferma a ...? [kwesto treno see fairma a]

arrive	arrivare [ar'reevareh]
child ticket	biglietto per ragazzi [beel-yet'to pair ragat'see]
compartment	compartimento [komparteemento]
connecting train	treno coincidente [treno ko-eencheedenteh], coincidenza [ko-eencheedent-sa]
departure,	partenza [parent-sa],
time of departure	orario di partenza [orar-yo dee parent-sa]
emergency brake	freno d'emergenza [freno demairjend-za]
engaged	occupato [ok'koopato]
fare	prezzo del biglietto [pret'so del beel-yet'to]
free/vacant	libero [leebairo]
get on (the train)	salire [saleereh]
get out	scendere [shendaireh]
Internet booking/printout	la prenotazione online/il biglietto cartaceo [la prenotat-syoneh onla-een/eel beel-yet'to kartachayo]
left-luggage/baggage locker	cassetta di sicurezza [kas'set'ta dee seekooret'sa]
left-luggage/baggage office	deposito bagagli [depozeeto bagal-yee]
luggage/baggage	bagaglio [bagal-yo]
main station	la stazione centrale [la stat-syoneh chentraleh]
motorail service	treno traghetto [treno traget'to]
non-smoking compartment	scompartimento per non fumatori [skomparteemento pair non foomatoree]
platform/track	banchina/binario [bankeena/beenar-yo]
power socket	connessione elettrica [kon'nes'syoneh elet'treeka]
reduction	la riduzione [la reedoot-syoneh]
restaurant/dining car	il vagone ristorante [eel vagoneh reestoranteh]
return ticket	biglietto di andata e ritorno [beel-yet'to dee andata eh reetorno]
seat reservation	prenotazione f posto [prenotat-syoneh posto]
sleeping car	vagone m letto [vagoneh let'to]
station	la stazione [la stat-syoneh]
stop (station)	fermata [fairmata]
supplement	supplemento [soop'plemento]
taken	occupato [ok'koopato]
ticket, ticket office	biglietto [beel-yet'to], biglietteria [beel-yet'tairee-ya]
timetable	orario [orar-yo]
toilet	gabinetto [gabeenet'to]
train	la ferrovia [la fair'rovee-ya]
waiting room	sala d'aspetto [sala daspet'to]
window seat	posto al finestrino [posto al feenestreeno]

TRAVELLING BY BOAT

AT THE PORT | AL PORTO [al porto]

When does the next ship leave for...?	Quando parte la prossima nave per …? [kwando parteh la pros'seema naveh pair]
How long does the crossing take?	Quanto dura la traversata? [kwanto doora la travairsata]
I'd like a ticket to...	Vorrei un biglietto per … [vor'ray oon beel-yet'to pair]
I'd like a ticket for the round trip at... o'clock.	Vorrei un biglietto per il giro delle … [vor'ray oon beel-yet'to pair eel jeero del'leh]
When do we arrive at...?	Quando attracchiamo a …? [kwando at'trak'kyamo a]

ON BOARD | A BORDO [a bordo]

Where's the restaurant/ lounge?	Dov'è la sala da pranzo/il salone? [doveh la sala da prand-zo/eel saloneh]
I don't feel well.	Non mi sento bene. [non mee sento beneh]
Could you give me something for seasickness, please.	Mi dia qualcosa contro il mal di mare, per favore. [mee dee-ya kwalkosa kontro eel mal dee mareh, pair favoreh]

cabin	cabina [kabeena]
captain	capitano [kapeetano]
car ferry/train ferry	autotraghetto/la nave traghetto [owtotraget'to/la naveh traget'to]
coast	costa [kosta]
deck	coperta [kopairta]
dock	approdo [ap'prodo]
excursion	l'escursione f a terra [leskoor-syoneh a tair'ra]
hovercraft	l'hovercraft m [lovairkraft]
life-jacket	giubbetto di salvataggio [joob'bet'to dee salvataj'jo]
lifebelt	il salvagente [eel salvajenteh]
lifeboat	scialuppa di salvataggio [sh-yaloop'pa dee salvataj'jo]
mainland	terra ferma [tair'ra fairma]
motorboat	motoscafo [motoskafo]
on board	a bordo [a bordo]
port	porto [porto]
rowing boat	barca a remi [barka a remee]
rough seas	moto ondoso [moto ondoso]
be seasick	avere il mal di mare [avaireh eel mal dee mareh]
ticket	biglietto [beel-yet'to]
wave	onda [onda]

PUBLIC TRANSPORT

BUS/UNDERGROUND
L'AUTOBUS/METROPOLITANA [lowtoboos/metropoleetana]

Excuse me, where's the nearest...	Dov'è la prossima ... [doveh la pros'seema]
bus stop?	fermata dell'autobus? [fairmata del'lowtoboos]
tram stop?	fermata del tram? [fairmata del tram]
underground station?	stazione della metropolitana? [stat-syoneh del'la metropoleetana]
Which line goes to...?	Qual è la linea che va a ...? [kwal eh la leenaya keh va a]
Where does the bus leave?	Da dove parte l'autobus? [da doveh parteh lowtoboos]
Where do I have to get out/ change?	Dove devo scendere/cambiare? [doveh devo shendaireh/kambyareh]
Will you tell me when we're there, please?	Senta, scusi, potrebbe avvertirmi quando devo scendere? [senta, skoozee, potreb'beh av'vairteermee kwando devo shendaireh]
Where can I buy a ticket?	Dove si comprano i biglietti? [doveh see komprano ee beel-yet'tee]
A ticket to..., please.	Un biglietto per ..., per favore. [oon beel-yet'to pair ..., pair favoreh]
Can I take a bicycle?	Posso portare la bicicletta? [pos'so portareh la beecheeklet'ta]
bus	l'autobus m [lowtoboos]
buy a ticket	comprare un biglietto [komprareh oon beel-yet'to]
departure	partenza [partent-sa]
driver	il conducente [eel kondoochenteh]
fare/ticket price	prezzo del biglietto [pret'so del beel-yet'to]
get on, get out	salire [saleereh], scendere [shendaireh]
inspector	il controllore [eel kontrol'loreh]
one-day travelcard	biglietto giornaliero [beel-yet'to jornal-yairo]

LOCAL KNOWLEDGE

biglietto

Inside Tip

Tickets, please!

If you want to take public transport in Italy and there isn't a ticket machine in sight, you'll need to buy your ticket at a nearby newspaper kiosk, tobacconist or stationery store.

stop	fermata [fairmata]
street, road	strada [strada], via [vee-ya]
terminus	il capolinea [eel kapoleenaya]
ticket	biglietto [beel-yet'to]
ticket machine	il distributore automatico di biglietti
	[eel deestreebootoreh owtomateeko dee beel-yet'tee]
timetable	orario [orar-yo]
tourist ticket	un biglietto per turisti [oon beel-yet'to pair tooreestee]
tram	il tram [eel tram]
underground	metropolitana [metropoleetana]
weekly season ticket	abbonamento settimanale [ab'bonamento set'teemanaleh]

TAXI | TASSÌ [tas'see]

Would you call a taxi for me, please?	Potrebbe chiamarmi un tassì?
	[potreb'beh kya-marmee oon tas'see]
Where's the nearest taxi rank?	Senta, scusi c'è un posteggio di tassì qui vicino?
	[senta, skoozee cheh oon postej'jo dee tas'see kwee veecheeno]
To the station.	Alla stazione. [al'la stat-syoneh]
To the... hotel.	All'albergo ... [al'lalbairgo]
To (name of street).	In via ... [een vee-ya]
To..., please.	A ..., per favore. [a ..., pair favoreh]
How much will it cost to...?	Quanto costa andare a ...? [kwanto kosta andareh a]
That's too much.	È troppo. [eh trop'po]
Could you stop here, please?	Si fermi qui. [see fairmee kwee]
That's for you.	Questo è per Lei. [kwesto eh pair lay]
I'd like a receipt, please.	La ricevuta, per favore. [la reechevoota, pair favoreh]

fare	prezzo del biglietto [pret'so del beel-yet'to]
taxi driver	il/la tassista [eel/la tas'seesta]
taxi rank	posteggio di taxi [postej'jo dee taksee]
tip/gratuity	mancia [mancha]

LIFT SHARING

Are you going to...?	Va a ...? [va a]
Could you give me a lift to...?	Mi dà un passaggio?
	[mee da oon pas'saj'jo]
I'd like to get out here.	Vorrei scendere qui. [vor'ray shendaireh kwee]
Thank you very much for the lift.	Grazie del passaggio.
	[grat-syeh del pas'saj'jo]

> A CULINARY ADVENTURE

Order with ease and tuck in with pleasure – foreign menus will never be an indecipherable mystery again.

GOING FOR A MEAL | ANDARE A MANGIARE [andareh a manjareh]

Excuse me, is there... here?	Scusi, mi potrebbe indicare ...? [skoozee, mee potreb'beh eendeekareh]
a good restaurant	un buon ristorante? [oon bwon reestoranteh]
a restaurant serving local specialities	un locale tipico? [oon lokaleh teepeeko]
Can I reserve a table for (four) for this evening, please?	Può riservarci per stasera un tavolo per (quattro) persone? [pwo reesairvarchee pair stasaira oon tavolo pair (kwat'tro) pairsoneh]
Is this table free?	È libero questo tavolo/questo posto? [eh leebairo kwesto tavolo/kwesto posto]

FOOD & DRINK

A table for (two/three), please.	Per favore, un tavolo per (due/tre) persone.
	[pair favoreh, oon tavolo pair (doo-eh/treh) pairsoneh]
Do you have a (non)smoking area?	Avete un'area (non) fumatori?
	[aveteh oon-ar-aya (non) foomatoree]
Where are the toilets, please?	Dove sono i servizi igienici?
	[doveh sono ee sairveet-see eejen-eechee]
Enjoy your meal!	Buon appetito! [bwon ap'peteeto]
Cheers!	Alla Sua salute! [al'la soo-a salooteh]
The food is/was great!	Il cibo è/era squisito! [eel cheebo eh/aira skweezeeto]
Do you mind if I smoke?	Le dà noia se fumo? [leh da noya seh foomo]

■ ORDERING | L'ORDINAZIQNE [lordeenat-syoneh] ■

Waiter, could I have...	Cameriere/a m/f, ... [kamair-yaireh]
the menu, please.	il menụ, per favore. [eel menoo, pair favoreh]
the drinks menu, please.	la lista delle bevande, per favore.
	[la leesta del'leh bevandeh, pair favoreh]
the wine list, please.	la lista dei vini, per favore. [la leesta day veenee, pair favoreh]
What can you recommend?	Che cosa mi raccomanda? [keh kosa mee rak'komanda]
I'll have...	Prendo ... [prendo]
I'm sorry but we've run out of...	Purtroppo il/la ... è finito. [poortrop'po eel/la ... eh feeneeto]
I'd like to try a local speciality.	Vorrei un piatto tipico della regione.
	[vor'ray oon pyat'to teepeeko del'la rejoneh]
I'm diabetic/vegetarian/vegan.	Sono diabẹtico/vegetariano/vegano.
	[sono dee-yabeteeko/vejetar-yano/vegano]
I'm allergic to... eggs/	Sono allẹrgico a ... l'uovo [lwovo]/
gluten/dairy products/	la glutẹina [la glootayna]/i latticini [eel lat'teecheenee]/
nuts.	le noci. [leh nochee]
What would you like to drink?	Che cosa desịdera da bere? [keh kosa deseedaira da baireh]
A glass of..., please.	Per favore, un bicchiẹre di ... [pair favoreh, oon beek'kyaireh dee]
A (half) bottle of..., please.	Per favore, una (mezza) bottịglia di ...
	[pair favoreh, oona (met'sa) bot'teel-ya dee]
Bring us..., please.	Ci porti, per favore ... [chee portee, pair favoreh]

■ COMPLAINTS | RECLAMI [reklamee] ■

The food is cold.	Il mangiare è freddo. [eel manjareh eh fred'do]
The meat has not been cooked enough.	La carne non è cotta bene. [la karneh non eh kot'ta beneh]
Have you forgotten my...?	Ha dimenticato il mio/la mia ...? [a deementeekato eel mee-yo/la mee-ya]
I didn't order that.	Non ho ordinato questo. [non o ordeenato kwesto]
Fetch the manager, please.	Mi chiạmi per favore il direttore/il proprietạrio! [mee kyamee pair favoreh eel deeret'toreh/eel propree-yetar-yo]

■ PAYING | PAGARE [pagareh] ■

Could I have the bill/check, please?	Il conto, per favore. [eel konto, pair favoreh]
Everything on one bill/check, please.	Tutto insiẹme. [toot'to een-syemeh]
Could I have a receipt, please?	Potrebbe darmi una ricevuta? [potreb'beh darmee oona reechevoota]
Separate bills/checks, please.	Conti separati, per favore. [kontee separatee, pair favoreh]

That's for you.	Questo è per Lei. [kwesto eh pair lay]
Keep the change.	Il resto è per Lei. [eel resto eh pair lay]
The food was excellent.	Il mangiare era ottimo! [eel manjareh aira ot'teemo]

boil v	bollire [bol'leereh]
breakfast	prima colazione f [preema kolat-syoneh] **> page 46**
children's portion	la mezza porzione [la met'sa port-syoneh]
cold	freddo [fred'do]
cook (chef), cook v	cuoco m [kwoko]/cuoca f [kwoka], cuocere [kwochaireh]
cup	tazza [tat'sa]
cutlery	le posate [leh pozateh]
fork, knife, spoon	forchetta [forket'ta], coltello [koltel'lo], cucchiaio [kook'kya-yo]

LOCAL KNOWLEDGE

Insider Tip

> ### Something for Every Appetite

You'll be spoilt for choice when you eat out in Italy. Here's a quick guide to help you navigate the nation's wonderful selection of eateries:

osteria [ostair-eeya] – traditional taverns serving local wines and simple fare. They've fallen out of favour somewhat recently and are being replaced by more refined **enoteca** [enoteka], where fine wines are sold to accompany fine food.

trattoria [trat'toreeya] – restaurants (usually family-run) serving homemade meals.

ristorante [reestoranteh] – more formal restaurants serving a large selection of dishes. You're usually expected to order a complete meal: start with a *primo* [preemo] course of pasta, rice or soup, move onto a *secondo* [sekondo] course of meat or fish, and finish up with fruit or a dessert. If you're after something lighter, you'd be better off going to a...

tavola calda [tavola kalda] – snack bars serving a variety of hot starters and light lunches – the food is usually eaten standing up.

bar [bar] – cafés where Italians drink their morning *cappuccino* [kap'poot'cheeno] and enjoy *caffè* (espresso) [kaf'feh (espres'so)], *latte macchiato* [lat'teh mak'kyato] and aperitifs throughout the day. Various snacks usually also feature on the menu. You pay at the till first (have some change ready when ordering!), then take your *scontrino* [skontreeno] ("receipt") to the bar to pick up your order. You can stand at the bar or take a seat: the prices given on the price list (*listino prezzi* [leesteeno pret'see]) only apply if you stand.

pub [pab] – if you fancy a beer, head along to one of the many Irish-style pubs that have sprung up in Italy since the 1990s.

paninoteca [paneenoteka] – sandwich bars where you can buy hot and cold *panini* [paneenee] with various fillings. They're generally favoured by a younger clientele.

deep-fried	fritto [freet'to]
dessert	il dessert [eel des'sairt], il dolce [eel dolcheh] **> page 51**
diabetic	diabetico [dee-yabeteeko]
dinner	cena [chena]
dish (course)	pietanza [pyetant-sa]
dish of the day	piatto del giorno [pyat'to del jorno]
drink	bevanda [bevanda] **> page 45, 52, 53**
fishbone	spina [speena], lisca [leeska]
fresh	fresco [fresko]
fried	fritto [freet'to]
garlic	aglio [al-yo]
glass	il bicchiere [eel beek'kyaireh]
gluten-free	senza glutine m [sent-sa glooteeneh]
gravy	salsa [salsa]
grilled	alla griglia [al'la greel-ya]
hot (spicy)	piccante [peek'kanteh]
hot (temperature)	caldo [kaldo], (very hot) bollente [bol'lenteh]
low-fat	con pochi grassi [kon pokee gras'see]
lunch	pranzo [prand-zo], il desinare [eel dezeenareh]
main course	secondo [sekondo] **> page 48, 49**
mustard	la senape [la senapeh]
napkin	tovagliolo [toval-yolo]
oil	olio [ol-yo]
order n	l'ordinazione f [lordeenat-syoneh]
pepper	il pepe [eel pepeh]
plate	piatto [pyat'to]
portion	la porzione [la port-syoneh]
rare (meat)	al sangue [al san-gweh]
raw	crudo [kroodo]
salt	il sale [eel saleh]
sauce	salsa [salsa]
seasoning	condimento [kondeemento]
soup	minestra [meenestra] **> page 46**
sour	agro [agro]
spice	le spezie [leh spet-syeh]
starter	antipasto [anteepasto] **> page 46**
sugar, (without) sugar	zucchero [tsook'kairo], (senza) zucchero [(sent-sa) tsook'kairo]
sweet	dolce [dolcheh]
tip/gratuity	mancia [mancha]
toothpick	lo stuzzicadenti [lo stoot'seeka-dentee]
vinegar	aceto [acheto]
waiter, waitress	il cameriere [eel kamair-yaireh], la cameriera [la kamair-yaira]
water	acqua [ak'kwa]
well-done (meat)	ben cotto [ben kot'to]

insalata
[eensalata]

i fagioli
[ee fajolee]

peperoncini m, pl **verdi**
[pepaironcheenee vairdee]

peperoni m, pl
[pepaironee]

pomodori m, pl
[pomodoree]

cetriolo
[chetree-yolo]

cavolfiore m
[kavol-fyoreh]

broccoli f
[brok'kolee]

carciofi m, pl
[karch-yofee]

funghi m, pl
[foon-gee]

melanzane f, pl
[meland-zaneh]

sedano
[sedano]

patate f, pl
[patateh]

cipolla
[cheepol'la]

aglio
[al-yo]

zenzero
[dzend-zairo]

l'avocado m
[lavokado]

carote f, pl
[karoteh]

cavolo
[kavolo]

porro
[por'ro]

asparagi m, pl
[asparajee]

lenticchie m, pl
[lenteek'kyeh]

zucca
[tsook'ka]

zucchini m, pl
[tsook'keenee]

piselli mpl
[peesel'lee]

i ceci
[ee chechee]

spinaci m, pl
[speenachee]

il mais/granturco
[eel ma-ees/grantoorko]

salvia
[salv-ya]

menta
[menta]

prezzemolo
[pret'semolo]

rosmarino
[rozmareeno]

le albicocche
[leh albeekok'keh]

le banane
[leh bananeh]

l'ananas m
[lananas]

mango
[man-go]

fragola
[fragola]

pesca
[peska]

il kiwi
[eel keewee]

l'uva f
[loova]

mela
[mela]

le pere
[leh paireh]

i mirtilli
[ee meerteel'lee]

le ciliegie
[leh cheel-yej-yeh]

i ribes
[ee reebes]

arancia
[arancha]

il limone
[eel leemoneh]

limetta
[leemet'ta]

papaia
[pa-pa-ya]

cocomero/anguria
[kokomairo/an-goor-ya]

il melone
[eel meloneh]

pompelmo
[pompelmo]

melagrana
[melagrana]

le prugne
[leh proon-yeh]

piccola susina mirabella
[peek'kola sooseena meerabel'ta]

i fichi
[ee feekee]

i litchi
[ee leechee]

pompelmo
[pompelmo]

la noce di cocco
[la nocheh dee kok'ko]

castagna/il marrone
[kastan-ya/eel mar'roneh]

le noccioline americane
[leh not'chyo-leeneh amaireekaneh]

i cranberries
[ee kran-bair'rees]

frutta secca
[froot'ta sek'ka]

frutta secca mista
[froot'ta sek'ka meesta]

il pane/il toast
[eel paneh/eel tohst]

il pane nero
[eel paneh nairo]

pane integrale
[paneh eentegraleh]

la baguette
[la ba-get]

il bagel
[eel bag-el]

il brezel
[eel bret-sel]

cornetto
[kornet'to]

le fette croccanti
[leh fet'teh krok'kantee]

focaccia
[fokat'cha]

i panini
[ee paneenee]

panino integrale
[paneeno eentegraleh]

il pumpernickel
[eel poom-pair-nee-kel]

il wafer/la cialda
[eel vafair/la chalda]

le ciambelline donut
[leh chambel'leeneh donoot]

pasta
[pasta]

il dolce/torta
[eel dolcheh/torta]

galletta di riso
[gal'let'ta dee reeso]

il müesli
[eel moo-ezlee]

i cornflakes
[ee kornflayks]

lo yogurt
[lo yo-goort]

burro
[boor'ro]

le uova
[leh wova]

formaggio
[formaj'jo]

formaggio tipo gorgonzola
[formaj'jo teepo gorgond-zola]

il camembert
[eel kamombair]

formaggio fresco
[formaj'jo fresko]

il latte
[eel lat'teh]

formaggio quark alle erbe
[formaj'jo kwark al'leh airbeh]

formaggio Bonbel
[formaj'jo bonbel]

parmigiano
[parmeejano]

pecorino
[pekoreeno]

manzo
[mand-zo]

le interiora/le frattaglie
[leh eentair-yora/leh frat'tal-yeh]

femminile/maschile
[fem'meeneeleh/maskeeleh]

vitello
[veetel'lo]

il maiale/suino
[eel ma-yaleh/soo-eeno]

agnello
[an-yel'lo]

pollo
[pol'lo]

anitra
[aneetra]

la lepre
[la lepreh]

il cinghiale
[eel cheeng-yaleh]

un pezzo di carne
[oon pet'so dee karneh]

carne f a dadi
[karneh a dadee]

la carne macinata
[la karneh macheenata]

gli spiedini di carne
[l-yee spyed-eenee dee karneh]

bistecca
[beestek'ka]

filetto
[feelet'to]

costoletta
[kostolet'ta]

il roastbeef
[eel rohst-beef]

i wurstel
[ee voorstel]

il salume
[eel saloomeh]

il salame
[eel salameh]

prosciutto cotto
[proshoot'to kot'to]

prosciutto crudo
[proshoot'to kroodo]

(smoked) lo speck [lo spek]
(dried) pancetta [panchet'ta]

pollo alla griglia
[pol'lo al'la greel-ya]

coscia di pollo
[kosh-ya dee pol'lo]

branzino
[brant-seeno]

trota
[trota]

tonno
[ton'no]

il salmone
[eel salmoneh]

le sardine
[leh sardeeneh]

i granchi
[ee grankee]

gli scampi
[l-yee skampee]

l'astice
[lasteecheh]

le cozze/vongole f, pl
[leh kot'seh/von-goleh]

i calamari
[ee kalamaree]

le ostriche
[leh ostreekeh]

il caviale
[eel kav-yaleh]

l'acqua minerale naturale
[lak'kwa meenairaleh natooraleh]

l'acqua minerale frizzante
[lak'kwa meenairaleh freet'santeh]

il latte
[eel lat'teh]

il latte di soia
[eel lat'teh dee soya]

succo/ spremuta
[sook'ko/spremoota]

coca
[koka]

bevanda energetica
[bevanda enairjeteeka]

birra
[beer'ra]

il tè
[eel teh]

caffè m
[kaf'feh]

cacao
[kakow]

cubetto di ghiaccio
[koobet'to dee gyat'ch-yo]

vino rosso
[veeno ros'so]

vino bianco
[veeno byanko]

lo spumante/champagne
[lo spoomanteh/shampan-yuh]

il cocktail
[eel kok-tayl]

PRIMA COLAZIONE [preema kolat-syoneh] | BREAKFAST

> Point & Show: page 43

il caffè amaro [eel kaf'feh amaro]	black coffee
il caffè all'americana [eel kaf'feh al'lamaireekana]	filter coffee
il caffellatte [eel kaf'fel'lat'teh]	coffee with milk
il caffè decaffeinizzato [eel kaf'feh dekaf'fayneet'sato]	decaffeinated coffee
il tè al latte/al limone [eel teh al lat'teh/al leemoneh]	tea with milk/lemon
bustina del tè [boosteena del teh]	tea bag
tisana [teezana]	herbal tea
cioccolata [chyok'kolata]	hot chocolate
spremuta [spremoota]	(freshly squeezed) lemon juice
uovo à la coque [wovo a la kok]	soft-boiled egg
uovo al tegamino [wovo al tegameeno]	fried egg
le uova strapazzate [leh wova strapat'sateh]	scrambled eggs
le uova con lo speck [leh wova kon lo spek]	eggs with ham
pane/panini/	bread/bun/
pane tostato [paneh/paneenee/paneh tostato]	toast
cornetto [kornet'to]	croissant (usually sweet)
burro [boor'ro]	butter
formaggio [formaj'jo]	cheese
i salume affettati [ee saloomeh af'fet'tatee]	cold cuts
prosciutto [proshoot'to]	ham
il miele [eel myeleh], **marmellata** [marmel'lata]	honey, jam/preserve/marmalade
lo yogurt [lo yogoort]	yoghurt
frutta [froot'ta]	fruit

ANTIPASTI [anteepastee] | STARTERS

acciughe/alici sott'olio [at'chyoogeh/aleecheh sot'tol-yo]	anchovies in oil
affettato misto [af'fet'tato meesto]	cold cuts
capesante [kapesanteh]	scallops
crostini [krosteenee]	slices of grilled bread with meat or vegetable toppings
fave e pecorino [faveh eh pekoreeno]	broadbeans with sheep's cheese
formaggi e marmellatine [formaj'jee eh marmel'lateeneh]	cheese with different preserves made from green tomatoes, onions, radicchio, etc.
funghi sott'olio [foon-gee sot'tol-yo]	mushrooms in oil
insalata di farro [eensalata dee far'ro]	spelt salad
pinzimonio [peent-seemon-yo]	raw vegetables served with a vinaigrette

prosciutto con melone/con fichi freschi dry cured, raw ham served with melon/
[proshoot'to kon meloneh/kon feekee freskee] fresh figs
prosciutto crudo [proshoot'to kroodo] dry cured ham
tonno con fagioli [ton'no kon fajolee] tuna and white beans

▪ PRIMI PIATTI [preemee pyat'tee] | PASTA AND RICE DISHES/SOUPS

spaghetti... [spaget'tee] spaghetti ...
 aglio, olio e peperoncino with garlic, olive oil and chili
 [al-yo, ol-yo eh pepaironcheeno]
 al burro/in bianco [al boor'ro/een byanko] with butter
 al cartoccio [al kartot'chyo] cooked and served in a parcel of
 baking paper, usually with fish sauce
 alla Bolognese/al ragù [al'la bolon-ye-seh/al ragoo] with minced meat sauce
 alla carbonara [al'la karbonara] with eggs and bacon
 alla napoletana [al'la napoletana] with tomato sauce (meat free)
 al pomodoro [al pomodoro] with tomato sauce
 alla puttanesca [al'la poot'taneska] with tomato sauce, olives and
 very hot spices
 alle vongole [al'leh von-goleh] with clams
 agnolotti/ravioli/tortellini filled pockets of pasta
 [an-yolot'tee/ravee-yolee/tortel'leenee]
cannelloni [kan'nel'lonee] baked rolls of pasta stuffed with a meat
 or vegetable filling
crespelle [krespel'leh] crêpes with meat or vegetable fillings
fettuccine/tagliatelle [fet'toot'cheeneh/tal-yatel'leh] pasta ribbons
lasagne al forno [lazan-yeh al forno] baked pasta dish with layers of meat,
 tomato sauce and cheese (lasagna)
rigatoni [reegatonee] ridged tubes of pasta
tagliatelle verdi [tal-yatel'leh vairdee] green pasta ribbons
trenette al pesto [trenet'teh al pesto] narrow pasta ribbons in a basil sauce
vermicelli [vairmeechel'lee] pasta threads
gnocchi al pomodoro [n-yok'kee al pomodoro] small potato dumplings in tomato sauce
polenta (alla valdostana) [polenta (al'la valdostana)] cornmeal porridge (with soft cheese)
risotto alla milanese [reesot'to al'la meelaneseh] risotto with saffron
risotto con funghi [reesot'to kon foon-gee] risotto with mushrooms
capelli d'angelo in brodo [kapel'lee danjelo een brodo] meat broth with pasta threads
crema di zucca [krema dee tsook'ka] cream of pumpkin soup
minestra di riso [meenestra dee reeso] rice soup
il minestrone [eel meenestroneh] thick vegetable soup
pasta e fagioli [pasta eh fajolee] thick soup with beans and pasta
stracciatella [strat'chatel'la] egg drop soup (soup with added egg)
zuppa di pane [tsoop'pa dee paneh] bread soup

zuppa di pesce [tsoop'pa dee pesheh] — fish soup
zuppa pavese [tsoop'pa paveseh] — meat broth with egg and toast

■CARNI [karnee] | MEAT DISHES

> Point & Show: page 44

agnello [an-yel'lo] — lamb
agnello di latte [an-yel'lo dee lat'teh] — roast lamb
anitra [aneetra] — duck
arrosto di vitello [ar'rosto dee veetel'lo] — roast veal
bistecca ai ferri [beestek'ka aee fair'ree] — grilled steak
bollito misto [bol'leeto meesto] — stew made from various meats
capretto [kapret'to] — kid goat
tagliata [tal-yata] — sliced rare steak
coniglio [koneel-yo] — rabbit
cotoletta alla milanese [kotolet'ta al'la meelaneseh] — breaded veal cutlet
cotoletta di maiale [kotolet'ta dee ma-yaleh] — pork cutlet
fegato [fegato] — liver
fesa di vitello [feza dee veetel'lo] — veal cutlet
la lepre [la lepreh] — hare
lingua [leen-gwa] — tongue
il maiale [eel ma-yaleh] — pork
lombata di vitello [lombata dee veetel'lo] — veal tenderloin
manzo/bue [mand-zo/boo-eh] — beef
il montone [eel montoneh] — mutton
oca [oka] — goose
ossobuco [os'sobooko] — cross-cut veal shanks in sauce
petti di pollo [pet'tee dee pol'lo] — chicken breasts
il piccione [eel peet'ch-yoneh] — pigeon
pollo [pol'lo] — chicken
pollo arrosto [pol'lo ar'rosto] — roast chicken
i rognoni [ee ron-yonee] — kidneys
i saltimbocca alla romana
  [ee salteembok'ka al'la romana] — small veal cutlets with ham and sage
le scaloppine di vitello
  [leh skalop'peeneh dee veetel'lo] — small veal cutlets
spezzatino [spet'sateeno] — (meat) stew with tomatoes
stufato [stoofato] — pot roast
tacchino [tak'keeno] — turkey
trippa [treep'pa] — tripe
vitello [veetel'lo] — veal
lo zampone [lo tsamponeh] — stuffed pig's trotter

PESCE E CROSTACEI [pesheh eh krostachay] | FISH AND SHELLFISH

> Point & Show: page 45

anguilla [an-gweel'la]	eel
aragosta [aragosta]	lobster
i calamari [ee kalamaree]	squid (calamari)
le cozze/vongole [leh kot'seh/von-goleh]	mussels
i datteri di mare [ee dat'tairee dee mareh]	date mussels
fritto di pesce [freet'to dee pesheh]	small fried fish
i frutti di mare [ee froot'tee dee mareh]	seafood selection
gambero [gambairo], **granchio** [grankyo]	prawn, crab
il pesce spada [eel pesheh spada]	swordfish
coda di rospo [koda dee rospo]	angler fish
passera di mare [pas'saira dee mareh]	flounder
polpo [polpo]	octopus
il salmone [eel salmoneh]	salmon
scampi fritti [skampee freet'tee]	(deep)fried shrimps or prawns
sgombro [zgombro]	mackerel
sogliola [sol-yola]	sole
triglia [treel-ya]	mullet
tonno [ton'no]	tuna
trota [trota]	trout

VERDURA E CONTORNI [vairdoora eh kontornee]
VEGETABLES AND SIDE DISHES

> Point & Show: page 41

gli asparagi [l-yee asparajee]	asparagus
bietola [byetola]	Swiss chard
i broccoli [ee brok'kolee]	broccoli
i carciofi [ee karch-yofee]	artichokes
le carote [leh karoteh]	carrots
il cavolfiore [eel kavol-fyoreh]	cauliflower
cavolo [kavolo]	cabbage
cipolla scalogna [cheepol'la skalon-ya]	shallots
le taccole [leh tak'koleh]	sugar peas
i fiori fritti [ee fyoree freet'tee]	(deep)fried courgette/zucchini flowers
cicoria belga [cheekor-ya belga]	chicory
i fagioli [ee fajolee], **i fagiolini** [ee fajoleenee]	white beans, green beans
finocchi [feenok'kee]	fennel
i funghi [ee foon-gee]	mushrooms

le lenticchie [leh lenteek'kyeh]	lentils
le melanzane [leh meland-zaneh]	aubergines
le patate [leh patateh]	potatoes
le patatine fritte [leh patateeneh freet'teh]	french fries/chips, fried potatoes
i peperoni [ee pepaironee]	(bell) peppers
i piselli [ee peesel'lee]	peas
i pomodori [ee pomodoree]	tomatoes
i ravanelli [ee ravanel'lee]	radishes
sedano [sedano]	celery
gli spinaci [l-yee speenachee]	spinach
gli zucchini [l-yee tsook'keenee]	courgette/zucchini

INSALATE [eensalateh] | SALADS

insalata mista/verde [eensalata meesta/ vairdeh]	mixed/green salad
radicchio [radeek'kyo]	radicchio (red, slightly bitter leaves)
scarola [skarola]	endives
valeriana [valairee-yana]	lamb's lettuce/corn salad (tangy leaves)

UOVA [wova] | EGG DISHES

frittata [freet'tata]	omelet, pancake
uova al tegame [wova al tegameh]	fried eggs
uova sode [wova sodeh]	hard boiled eggs
uova strapazzate [wova strapat'sateh]	scrambled eggs

FORMAGGI [formaj'jee] | CHEESE

 Point & Show: page 43

bel paese [bel pa-yezeh]	mild, semi-soft cheese
gorgonzola [gorgond-zola]	veined, strong blue cheese
gruviera [groov-yaira]	hard, yellow cheese (gruyère)
mozzarella [mot'sarel'la]	fresh buffalo-milk cheese
parmigiano/grana [parmeejano/grana]	parmesan cheese
pecorino [pekoreeno]	sheep's cheese
provolone (affumicato) [provoloneh (af'foomeekato)]	strong, semi-hard (smoked) cheese
ricotta [reekot'ta]	soft, unsalted white cheese
stracchino [strak'keeno]	mild, spreadable cheese
taleggio [talej'jo]	white, semi-soft, mild cheese

DOLCI E FRUTTA [dolchee eh froot'ta] | DESSERTS AND FRUIT

> Point & Show: page 42

budino [boodeeno]	pudding
crème caramel [krem karamel]	caramel pudding
cassata [kas'sata]	filled cake with candied fruit
gelato [jelato]	ice cream
macedonia [machedon-ya]	fruit salad
tiramisu [teerameesoo]	coffee-flavoured dessert
zabaione [dzaba-yoneh]	whipped custard dessert with sweet wine
zuppa inglese [tsoop'pa een-gleseh]	Italian trifle: custard-based dessert with cake or soft biscuits
albicocca [albeekok'ka]	apricot
arancia [arancha]	orange
ciliegie [cheel-yej-yeh]	cherries
cocomero/anguria [kokomairo/an-goor-ya]	watermelon
fichi [feekee]	figs
fragole [fragoleh]	strawberries
lamponi [lamponee]	raspberries
mela [mela]	apple
melone [meloneh]	melon
mirtilli rossi [meerteel'lee ros'see]	cranberries
pera [paira]	pear
pesca [peska]	peach
prugna/susina [proon-ya/sooseena]	plum
uva [oova]	grapes

GELATI [jelatee] | ICE CREAMS

albicocca [albeekok'ka]	apricot
coppa assortita [kop'pa as'sorteeta]	mixed ice cream sundae
coppa con panna [kop'pa kon pan'na]	ice cream sundae with cream
fior di latte [fyor dee lat'teh]	ice cream made with semi-soft cheese
fragola [fragola]	strawberry
lampone [lamponeh]	raspberry
limone [leemoneh]	lemon
mirtilli [meerteel'lee]	blueberry
nocciola [not'chyola]	hazelnut
tartufo [tartoofo]	vanilla ice cream with a chocolate shell
vaniglia/crema [vaneel-ya/krema]	vanilla

BEVANDE ANALCOLICHE [bevandeh analkoleekeh]
SOFT DRINKS

acqua minerale [ak'kwa meenairaleh]	mineral water
acqua di seltz [ak'kwa dee selts]	soda water
amarena [amarena]	cherry juice
aranciata [aranchata]	orange soda
gassosa [gas'sosa]	soda
spremuta di limone [spre-moota dee leemoneh]	freshly squeezed lemon juice
succo di frutta [sook'ko dee froot'ta]	fruit juice

CAFFETTERIA [kaf'fet'tairee-ya] | IN THE CAFÉ

il caffè [eel kaf'feh], **espresso** [espres'so]	small, strong coffee without milk
il caffè macchiato [eel kaf'feh mak'kyato]	small, strong coffee with milk
cappuccino [kap'poot'cheeno]	coffee with frothy milk
camomilla [kamomeel'ta]	cammomile tea
il tè al latte/limone [eel teh al lat'teh/leemoneh]	tea with milk/lemon
cioccolata con panna [chyok'kolata kon pan'na]	hot chocolate with whipped cream

VINI [veenee] | WINES

Aleatico [alayateeko]	a sweet red wine from Tuscanny
Asti Spumante [astee spoomanteh]	a sparkling wine from Piedmont
Barbera [barbaira]	a light, tart red wine from Piedmont
Bardolino [bardoleeno]	a fresh red wine from the Lake Garda region
Chianti [kyantee]	a fruity red wine from Tuscany
Frascati [fraskatee]	a not overly sweet white wine (from the Castelli Romani)
Grignolino [green-yoleeno]	a light, floral red wine from Piedmont
Làcrima Christi [lakreema kreestee]	a harmonious red wine from Naples
Lambrusco [lambroosko]	a sparkling red wine (Modena-Bologna)
Marino [mareeno]	a dry white wine from the Castelli Romani
Marsala [marsala]	a dark, sweet fortified wine from Sicily
Moscato [moskato]	a sweet Italian dessert wine
Orvieto [orv-yeto]	an Umbrian white wine (with sweet and dry varieties)
Ruffino [roof'feeno]	a red wine from Tuscany
Valpolicella [valpoleechel'la]	a red wine from Verona

THE DRINKS MENU

BIRRE [beer'reh] | BEER

birra scura/chiara [beer'ra skoora/kyara]   dark/light beer
birra forte/birra alla spina   strong, malty beer/draught beer
[beer'ra forteh/beer'ra al'la speena]

LIQUORI [leekworee] | LIQUEURS

amaro [amaro]   bitter-sweet herbal liqueur
grappa [grap'pa]   clear pomace (grape pulp) brandy
sambuca [sambooka]   aniseed-flavoured liqueur
Vecchia Romagna [vek'kya roman-ya]   Italian brandy

LOCAL KNOWLEDGE

Insider Tips

Don't Make a Meal of It

It doesn't matter how early you get up in the morning, it would be utterly unthinkable for an Italian to eat their evening meal before 7.30–8pm – even at the weekends or on holiday. And the further south you go, the later everyone eats.

Take Cover

If you sit down to eat in Italy, you'll usually see a *coperto* [kopairto] ("cover charge") listed on the menu. You always have to pay this fee, regardless of how much you order. In return, you won't pay a thing for the breads and *grissini* [grees'seenee] ("breadsticks") that will be brought to your table.

Tipping the Balance

Tipping really isn't necessary in Italy. If you'd like to reward a waiter or taxi driver for exceptional service, then go ahead, but don't feel obliged. You should also bear in mind that some restaurants will add a service charge to your bill.

Caffè ≠ Coffee!

Coffee lovers beware: if you order a *caffè* [kaf'feh] in Italy, you won't get your usual cup of Joe – you'll be served an espresso instead. There are a number of varieties of this diminutive drink to discover: a *caffè doppio* [kaf'feh dop'pyo] is two *espressi* [espres'see], a *caffè lungo* [kaf'feh loongo] is an espresso with extra hot water, a *caffè macchiato* [kaf'feh mak'kyato] is served with a little milk, and a *caffè corretto* [kaf'feh kor'ret'to] is drunk with a shot of alcohol (grappa, sambuca, etc.) And if you usually enjoy a *cappucino* [kap'poocheeno] in the afternoon, think twice: Italians never drink these frothy creations after 11am.

> SUCCESSFUL SHOPPING

Whether you're after chic shoes, the perfect souvenir, a toothbrush or some wholemeal bread, we've equipped you for every eventuality. We've also provided some very handy 'point & show' pictures.

■ AT THE SHOPS | AL NEGOZIO [al negot-syo]

Thanks. I'm just looking around.	Grazie, volevo solo dare un'occhiata. [grat-syeh, volevo solo dareh oon-ok'kyata]
Where can I find...?	Dove si può trovare ...? [doveh see pwo trovareh]
I'd like...	Vorrei ... [vor'ray]
Have you got...?	Ha ...? [a]
Do you take credit cards?	Accetta carte di credito? [at'chet'ta karteh dee kredeeto]
How much is it?	Quanto costa? [kwanto kosta]
That's a bit expensive!	Ma è caro! [ma eh karo]

SHOPPING

Is there any chance of a discount?	Può farmi uno sconto? [pwo farmee oono skonto]
The maximum I'm prepared to pay is...	Pago al massimo … [pago al mas'seemo]
I'll take it/them.	Lo prendo. [lo prendo]
Can you recommend a... shop?	Mi può indicare un negozio di …? [mee pwo eendeekareh oon negot-syo dee]

OPENING HOURS ORARIO D´APERTURA [orar-yo dapairtoora]
open, closed aperto [apairto], chiuso [kyooso]
closed for holidays/vacation chiuso per ferie [kyooso pair fair-yeh]

■SHOPS | NEGOZI [negot-see]

ufficio turistico
[oof'feechyo tooreesteeko]

ufficio postale
[oof'feechyo postaleh]

farmacia
[farmacha]

profumeria
[profoomairee-ya]

panificio
[panee-feech-yo]

fruttivendolo
[froot'teevendolo]

macelleria
[machel'lairee-ya]

negozio di calzature
[negot-syo dee kalt-satooreh]

ottico
[ot'teeko]

gioielleria
[joyel'tairee-ya]

pelletteria
[pel'let'tairee-ya]

l'elettricista m
[lelet'treecheesta]

giornalaio
[jornala-yo]

negozio di cellulari
[negot-syo dee chel'loolaree]

libreria
[leebrairee-ya]

negozio di dischi
[negot-syo dee deeskee]

negozio di giocattoli
[negot-syo dee jokat'to-lee]

fiaschetteria
[fyasket'tairee-ya]

gli articoli sportivi
[l-yee arteekolee sporteevee]

tabaccaio
[tabak'ka-yo]

fioraio
[fyora-yo]

il parrucchiere
[eel par'rook'kyaireh]

articoli m, pl casalinghi
[arteekolee kasaleen-gee]

agenzia viaggi
[ajent-see-ya vee-yaj'jee]

gli articoli fotografici
[l-yee arteekolee
fotografeechee]

negozio specializzato
in computer
[negot-syo spechaleet'sato
een kompootair]

rivendita di prodotti alcolici/
bottiglieria
[reevendeeta dee prodot'tee
alkoleechee/bot'teel-yair-ee-ya]

negozio di prodotti
biodinamici
[negot-syo dee prodot'tee
byodee-nameechee]

department store	il grande magazzino [eel grandeh magat'seeno]
flea market	mercato delle pulci [mairkato del'leh poolchee]
market	mercato [mairkato]
shopping centre/mall	centro commerciale [chentro kom'mairch-yaleh]
souvenir shop	negozio di souvenir [negot-syo dee sooveneer]
supermarket	supermercato [soopair-mair-kato]

SHOPPING

THE PHARMACY | FARMACIA [farmacha]

> At the Doctor's: page 107

Where's the nearest pharmacy?	Dov'è la farmacia piú vicina? [doveh la farmacha pyoo veecheena]
Can you give me something for...	Mi dia qualcosa contro …, per favore. [mee dee-ya kwalkosa kontro …, pair favoreh]

TAKE... PRENDERE ... [prendaireh ...]

internally	interno [pair oozo eentairno]
externally	esterno [estairno], esteriore [estair-yoreh]
on an empty stomach	a stomaco vuoto [a stomako vwoto]
before meals	prima dei pasti [preema day pastee]
after meals	dopo i pasti [dopo ee pastee]
let it dissolve in your mouth	far sciogliere in bocca [far shyol-yaireh een bok'ka]

> Further information: page 60

LOCAL KNOWLEDGE

Insider Tips

Keep the Receipt

Always hang on to your receipts! To crack down on tax fraud, the Italian police can carry out spot checks on consumers. If you're stopped within 100 metres of an establishment and you don't have a receipt (ricevuta fiscale [reechevoota feeskaleh]) for your purchase, then you could land the seller – and, technically, even yourself! – in hot water.

A Blue Haze

Only licenced bars and specialist shops are authorised to sell tobacco. You'll recognize them by the large blue signs emblazoned with a white "T" next to the entrance.

Chemist's/Drugstores

Italians don't have any shops that correspond to our chemists'/drug stores – if you want to buy everyday toiletries and general health products, you'll find them in supermarkets (*supermercato* [soopair-mairkato]), perfumeries (*profumeria* [profoomeree-ya]), pharmacies (*farmacia* [farma-chee-ya]) and home-ware stores (*mesticheria* [mesteekairee-ya], *casalinghi* [kasaleengee]).

il sapone
[eel saponeh]

il deodorante
[eel dayodoranteh]

crema
[krema]

carta igienica
[karta eej-yeneeka]

spazzolino da denti
[spat'soleeno da dentee]

dentifricio
[denteefreech-yo]

filo interdentale
[feelo eentairdentaleh]

i fazzoletti di carta
[ee fat'solet'tee dee karta]

lo shampoo
[lo shampoo]

la frizione
[la freet-syoneh]

il pettine/spazzola per i capelli
[eel pet'teeneh/spat'sola pair ee kapel'lee]

specchio
[spek'kyo]

limetta
[leemet'ta]

le pinzette
[leh peent-set'teh]

le forbici per le unghie
[leh forbeechee pair leh oong-yeh]

profumo
[profoomo]

il tampone
[eel tamponeh]

gli assorbenti
[l-yee as'sorbentee]

il mascara
[eel maskara]

rossetto
[ros'set'to]

la lametta
[la lamet'ta]

rasoio
[rasoyo]

la lozione dopobarba
[la lot-syoneh dopobarba]

i preservativi/profilattico
[ee presairvateevee/profeelat'teeko]

crema solare
[krema solareh]

borsa dell'acqua calda
[borsa del'lak'kwa kalda]

cerotto
[chairot'to]

tappo per le orecchie
[tap'po pair leh or'rek'kee-yeh]

ago
[ago]

filo
[feelo]

spillo di sicurezza
[speel'lo dee seekooret'sa]

il bottone
[eel bot'toneh]

ELECTRICAL GOODS/COMPUTING/PHOTOGRAPHY
APPARECCHI ELETTRICI/COMPUTER/FOTOGRAFIA

lampadina tascabile
[lampadeena taskabeeleh]

lampadina (ad incandescenza)
[lampadeena (ad eenkandeshent-sa)]

batteria
[bat'tairee-ya]

l'adattatore m
[ladat'tatoreh]

il computer portatile
[eel kompootair portateeleh]

cavo ricarica
[kavo reekareeka]

il CD/il DVD
[eel chee-dee/eel dee-voo-dee]

il chiavetta
[eel kyavet'ta]

la stampante
[la stampanteh]

lo scannerizzatore
[lo skan'nairee'satoreh]

il cellulare/telefonino
[eel chel'loolareh/telefoneeno]

cavo ricarica (cellulare)
[kavo reekareeka (chel'loolareh)]

il televisore
[eel televeezoreh]

la radio
[la rad-yo]

il let'toreh mp3/iPod
[eel let'toreh emeh-pee-tree/aee-pod]

cuffia
[koof'fya]

macchina fotografica digitale
[mak'keena fotografeeka deejeetaleh]

teleobiettivo
[telay-obyet'teevo]

accumulatore m
[ak'koomoolatoreh]

scheda di memoria
[skeda dee memor-ya]

il film
[eel feelm]

diapositiva
[dee-yapozeeteeva]

macchina fotografica
[mak'keena fotografeeka],
cinepresa subacquea
[cheenepresa soobak'kway-a]

cinepresa
[cheenepresa]

sveglia
[zvel-ya]

rasoio elettrico
[rasoyo elet'treeko]

spazzolino elettrico
[spat'soleeno elet'treeko]

il fon
[eel fon]

antibiotics	antibiotico [anteebyoteeko]
antidote	antidoto [anteedoto]
aspirin	aspirina [aspeereena]
burn ointment	pomata per le scottature [pomata pair leh skot'tatooreh]
camomile tea	camomilla [kamomeel'la]
circulatory stimulant	medicamento per disturbi circolatori [medeekamento pair deestoorbee cheerkolatoree]
condom	preservativo [presairvateevo], profilattico [profeelat'teeko]
contraceptive pill, morning-after pill	le pillole anticoncezionali [leh peel'loleh anteekonchet-syonalee], la pillola del giorno dopo [la peel'lola del jorno dopo]
cough mixture	sciroppo (contro la tosse) [sheerop'po (kontro la tos'seh)]
disinfectant	il disinfettante [eel deezeenfet'tanteh]
drops	le gocce [leh got'cheh]
ear drops	le gocce per gli orecchi [leh got'cheh pair l-yee orek'kee]
eye drops	le gocce per gli occhi [leh got'cheh pair l-yee ok'kee], collirio [kol'leer-yo]
gauze	fascia di garza [fash-ya dee gard-za]
headache tablets	le compresse contro il mal di testa [leh kompres'seh kontro eel mal dee testa]
insect repellent	l'insetticida m [leenset'teecheeda]
insulin	insulina [eensooleena]
(tincture of) iodine	tintura di iodio [teentoora dee yod-yo]
laxative	lassativo [las'sateevo]
medicine	medicina [medeecheena], farmaco [farmako]
mouthwash	la soluzione per gargarismi [la soloot-syoneh pair gargareezmee]
ointment	pomata [pomata]
painkillers	le compresse contro il dolore [leh kompres'seh kontro eel doloreh], gli analgesici [l-yee anal-jez-eechee]
powder	cipria [cheepree-ya], borotalco [borotalko]
prescription	ricetta [reechet'ta]
remedy	medicina [medeecheena]
sedative, tranquilizer	il calmante [eel kalmanteh]
side effects	le reazioni secondarie [leh rayat-syonee sekondar-yeh]
sleeping tablets	i sonniferi [ee son'neefairee]
sticking plasters/ adhesive bandages	cerotto [chairot'to]
stomach pain relief	digestivo in gocce [deejesteevo een got'cheh]
sunburn	scottatura (solare) [skot'tatoora (solareh)]
suppositories	supposta [soop'posta]
tablet/pill	compressa [kompres'sa]
thermometer	termometro [tairmometro]
throat lozenges	le pastiglie per la gola [leh pasteel-yeh pair la gola]

SHOPPING

■THE HAIRDRESSER'S | IL PARRUCCHIERE [eel par'rook'kyaireh] ■

Can I make an appointment for tomorrow?	Posso prendere un appuntamento per domani? [pos'so prendaireh oon ap'poontamento pair domanee]
Wash and cut/dry cut, please.	Tagliare e/senza lavare, per favore. [tal-yareh eh/sent-sa lavareh, pair favoreh]
A bit shorter.	Un po' più corti. [oon po pyoo kortee]
Not too short.	Non troppo corti. [non trop'po kortee]
Very short, please.	Molto corti, per favore. [molto kortee, pair favoreh]
I'd like a shave, please.	La barba, per favore. [la barba, pair favoreh]
Would you trim my beard, please.	Mi spunti la barba, per favore. [mee spoontee la barba, pair favoreh]
Thank you. That's fine.	Grazie. Va bene così. [grat-syeh va beneh kosee]

beard	barba [barba]
blond	biondo [byondo]
blow dry v	asciugare con il fon [ashoogareh kon eel fon]
colour/dye v	tingere [teenjaireh]
comb v	pettinare [pet'teenareh]
curls	i ricci [ee reet'chee]
cut the ends	tagliare le punte [tal-yareh leh poonteh]
dandruff	forfora [forfora]
do someone's hair	pettinare [pet'teenareh]
fringe	frangetta [franjet'ta]
hair	i capelli [ee kapel'lee]
haircut, hairstyle	taglio [tal-yo], pettinatura [pet'teenatoora]

LOCAL KNOWLEDGE

Insider Tip

Pampering

Italy is still home to the classic barbershop where you'll be sat down and given a shave in the age-old way: with a brush and cut-throat razor. From Treviso in the north right down to Palermo in the south, these establishments also offer a relaxing range of other services, including face and head massages, hair thickening and lengthening treatments, and a great deal more besides.

Female customers who have a grasp of Italian won't just be treated to a haircut: the barbers' shops are usually well stocked with a selection of relentlessly kitschy romantic photo novels laid out for your reading (dis!)pleasure.

highlights	ciocca di capelli [chyok'ka dee kapel'lee],
	(coloured) le mèches [leh mesh]
layers	capelli scalati [kapel'lee skalatee]
moustache	i baffi [ee baf'fee]
parting	riga [reega]
pluck (your) eyebrows	depilare le sopracciglia [depeelareh leh soprat'cheel-ya]
straighten	stirare [steerareh]

■ CLOTHING | ABBIGLIAMENTO [ab'beel-yamento] ■

Can you show me...?	Mi può mostrare … ? [mee pwo mostrareh]
Can I try it on?	Posso provarlo? [pos'so provarlo]
What size do you take?	Che taglia porta? [keh tal-ya porta]
It's too small/big.	Questo mi è troppo piccolo/grande.
	[kwesto mee eh trop'po peek'kolo/grandeh]
It's a good fit. I'll take it.	Va bene. Lo prendo. [va beneh lo prendo]
It's not quite what I wanted.	Non è proprio quello che volevo.
	[non eh propree-yo kwel'lo keh volevo]
Do you have it in a different colour?	Ce l'ha anche di un altro colore?
	[cheh la ankeh dee oon altro koloreh]
Thank you, I'll have to think about it.	Grazie, devo ripensarci un po'.
	[grat-syeh, devo reepensarchee oon po]

LOCAL
KNOWLEDGE

Inside Tips

▶ Don't Panic!

It's not uncommon to feel out of your depth when faced with foreign clothing sizes.
But never fear! Keep the following tricks in mind, and you'll be sure to get the right size whenever you hit the shops.

To work out your clothes size, use the following calculations: UK women: subtract 32 from the Italian size to get the UK size (e.g. an Italian size 42 = a UK size 10); US women: subtract 34 from the Italian size to get the US size (e.g. an Italian size 42 = a US size 8).

Men have it easier when it comes to the mathematics: UK/US men (coats, suits, etc.): subtract 10 from the Italian size to get your UK/US size (e.g. an Italian size 42 = UK/US size 32).

▶▶ "It fits like a Glove!"

It may be confusing to work out your size, but when you've found the perfect fit, the Italians have the same expression: *calza come un guanto* [kalt-sa komeh oon gwanto].

maglietta
[mal-yet'ta]

il pullover/il maglione
[eel pool-ovair/eel mal-yoneh]

maglia con cappuccio
[mal-ya kon kap'poot'chyo]

giacca
[jak'ka]

i pantaloni/i calzoni
[ee pantalonee/ee kalt-sonee]

i pantaloncini/gli shorts
[ee pantaloncheenee/l-yee shorts]

gonna
[gon'na]

cintura
[cheentoora]

camicetta
[kameechet'ta]

camicia
[kameecha]

giacca
[jak'ka]

giacca di lana/il golf
[jak'ka dee lana/eel golf]

abito
[abeeto]

vestito
[vesteeto]

il tailleur
[eel ta-yuhr]

cappotto/soprabito
[kap'pot'to/soprabeeto]

il collant/calzamaglia
[eel kol'lon/kalt-samal-ya]

biancheria intima
[byankairee-ya eenteema]

accappatoio
[ak'kap'patoyo]

i calzini/le calze
[ee kalt-seenee/leh kalt-seh]

il costume da bagno
[eel kostoomeh da ban-yo]

il costume da bagno
[eel kostoomeh da ban-yo]

il bikini
[eel beekeenee]

berretto
[bair'ret'to]

cappello
[kap'pel'lo]

i guanti
[ee gwantee]

lo scialle/sciarpa
[lo shyal'leh/sh-yarpa]

> You'll find an extensive list of culinary delights in the FOOD & DRINK chapter
> starting on page 41.

What's that?	Che cos'è? [keh koseh]
Can I try it?	Posso provarlo/la m/f [pos'so provarlo/la]
Do you sell ...?	Vendete ...? [vendeteh]
ECO products?	prodotti biologici [prodot'tee beeyo-lo-jeechee]
local products?	prodotti regionali [prodot'tee rejonalee]
I'd like...	Mi dia ..., per favore. [mee dee-ya ..., pair favoreh]
a pound (500 g) of...	mezzo chilo ... [met'so keelo], un chilo di ... [oon keelo dee]
a piece of...	un pezzo di ... [oon pet'so dee]
a packet of...	un pacco di ... [oon pak'ko dee]
a tin of...	una scatola di ..., [oona skatola dee]
a bottle of...	una bottiglia di ... [oona bot'teel-ya dee]
Thanks, that's everything.	Nient'altro, grazie. [nyent-altro, grat-syeh]

beverages/drinks	bevande m, pl [bevandeh] > page 45, 52
bread	il pane [eel paneh] > page 43, 46
butter	burro [boor'ro] > page 43, 46
cheese	formaggio [formaj'jo] > page 43, 50
chocolate	cioccolata [chyok'kolata]
coffee	il caffè [eel kaf'feh] > page 46, 52
cream	panna [pan'na]
dairy products	i latticini [ee lat'teecheenee] > page 43
eggs	le uova [leh wova] > page 43, 46
fish	il pesce [eel pesheh] > page 45, 49
flour	farina [fareena]
fresh	fresco [fresko]
fruit	la frutta [la froot'ta] > page 42, 51

LOCAL KNOWLEDGE

Inside Tip

> **Please Take a Number!**

When you're going shopping for food (at the baker's, the butcher's, etc.), make sure
to take a number from the shop's ticket machine as soon as you arrive. You'll be able
to judge roughly how long you'll have to wait by looking at the digital sign over the
counter – leaving you free to enjoy browsing elsewhere in the meantime.

ice cream	gelato [jelato] > page 51
jam	marmellata [marmel'lata] > page 46
margarine	margarina [margareena]
meat	la carne [la karneh] > page 44, 48
milk	il latte [eel lat'teh] > page 43
noodles	pasta [pasta]
oil	olio [ol-yo]
organic food	cibo biologico [cheebo byolojeeko]
patisserie (cakes and pastries)	pane m e pasticceria [paneh eh pasteet'chairee-ya] > page 43, 46
pepper	il pepe [eel pepeh]
(without) preservatives	(senza) conservanti [(sent-sa) konsairvantee]
salt	il sale [eel saleh]
sausage	le salsicce [leh salseet'cheh]
(without) sugar	(senza) zucchero [(sent-sa) tsook'kairo]
sweets	i dolciumi [ee dolch-yoomee]
vegetables	verdura [vairdoora] > page 41, 49, 50
vinegar	aceto [acheto]

■ THE OPTICIAN'S | OTTICO [ot'teeko]

Could you repair/adjust these glasses for me, please?	Mi potrebbe aggiustare, questi occhiali, per favore? [mee potreb'beh aj'joostareh, kwestee ok'kyalee, pair favoreh]
I'm short-sighted/ long-sighted.	Sono miope/presbite. [sono mee-yopeh/prezbeeteh]
What's your prescription?	Che capacità visiva ha? [keh kapacheeta veezeeva a]
in the right eye…/	destra … [destra], sinistra … [seeneestra];
in the left eye…	(plus/minus) più/meno [pyoo/meno]
I need some…	Ho bisogno di … [o beezon-yo dee]
soaking solution	soluzione per la conservazione [soloot-syoneh pair la konsairvat-syoneh]
cleansing solution	soluzione detergente [soloot-syoneh detairjenteh]
for hard/soft contact lenses.	per lenti a contatto rigide/morbide. [pair lentee a kontat'to reejeedeh/morbeedeh]
I'm looking for…	Vorrei … [vor'ray]
daily disposable lenses.	delle lenti a ricambio giornaliero. [del'leh lentee a reekambyo jornal-yairo]
some sunglasses.	un paio di occhiali da sole. [oon pa-yo dee ok'kyalee da soleh]

■ THE JEWELLER'S | DAL GIOIELLIERE [dal joyel'l-yaireh]

My watch doesn't work. Could you have a look at it?	Il mio orologio non va più. Potrebbe darci un'occhiata? [eel mee-yo orolojo non va pyoo potreb'beh darchee oonok'kyata]

I'd like a nice souvenir/ present.	Vorrei un bel souvenir/regalo. [vor'ray oon bel sooveneer/regalo]

bracelet	braccialetto [brat'chalet'to]
brooch	spilla [speel'la]
costume jewellery	bigiotteria [beejot'tairee-ya]
crystal	cristallo [kreestal'lo]
earrings	gli orecchini [l-yee orek'keenee]
genuine	vero [vairo]
gold	oro [oro]
jewellery	gioiello [joyel'lo]
necklace	collana [kol'lana], catena [katena]
pearl	perla [pairla]
pendant	ciondolo [chyondolo]
ring	anello [anel'lo]
silver	argento [arjento]
(precious) stone	pietra (preziosa) [pyetra (pret-syosa)]
waterproof	impermeabile [eempair-maya-beeleh]
wristwatch	orologio da polso [orolojo da polso]

■THE SHOE SHOP | NEGOZIO DI CALZATURE [nogot-syo dee kalt-satooreh]

I'd like a pair of...	Senta, vorrei un paio di scarpe da … [senta, vor'ray oon pa-yo dee skarpeh da]
I take a size...	Ho il numero … [o eel noomairo]
They're too narrow/broad.	Sono troppo strette/larghe. [sono trop'po stret'teh/largeh]

boots	gli stivali [l-yee steevalee]
gum/rubber boot, wellies	stivale m di gomma [steevaleh dee gom'ma]
(with) heels	(con) il tacco [(kon) eel tak'ko]
hiking boot	scarpa da trekking [skarpa da trek'keeng]
ladies'/men's shoe	scarpa da donna/uomo [skarpa da don'na/womo]
leather/rubber sole	suola di cuoio/gomma [swola dee kwoyo/gom'ma]
moccasin, sandals	mocassino [mokas'seeno], i sandali [ee sandalee]
trainers	le scarpe da ginnastica [leh skarpeh da jeen'nasteeka]

■SOUVENIRS | SOUVENIR [sooveneer]

I'd like...	Vorrei … [vor'ray]
a nice souvenir.	un bel souvenir. [oon bel sooveneer]
something that's typical of this region.	un oggetto tipico della zona. [oon oj'jet'to teepeeko del'la dzona]

I'd like something that's not too expensive.	Vorrei spendere il giusto. [vor'ray spendaireh eel joosto]
That's lovely.	Questo sì che è carino. [kwesto see keh eh kareeno]
Can you gift wrap it for me, please?	Potrebbe farmi un pacchetto regalo? [potreb'beh farmee oon pak'ket'to regalo]
Thanks, but I didn't find anything (I liked).	Grazie, ma non ho trovato niente (che mi piaccia). [grat-syeh, ma non o trovato nyenteh (keh mee pyat'cha)]

ceramics/pottery	ceramica [chairameeka]/il vasellame [eel vazel'lameh]
genuine	vero [vairo]
hand-made	lavorato a mano [lavorato a mano]
jewellery	gioiello [joyel'lo]
local products, local specialities	i prodotti regionali [ee prodot'tee rejonalee], le specialità regionali [leh spechaleeta rejonalee]
textiles	tessuti m, pl [tes'sootee]
wood sculptures/carvings	intaglio [eental-yo]

STATIONERY AND BOOKS | CANCELLERIA E LIBRI [kanchel'lairee-ya eh leebree] ▪

I'd like...	Vorrei ... [vor'ray]
an English newspaper.	un giornale inglese. [oon jornaleh een-gleseh]
a magazine.	una rivista. [oona reeveesta]
a travel guide.	una guida turistica. [oona gweeda tooreesteeka]
a novel in English.	un romanzo inglese. [oon romand-zo een-gleseh]

ballpoint pen/biro	la biro [la beero]
cookbook	libro di cucina [leebro dee koocheena]
envelope	busta [boosta]
eraser, glue	gomma [gom'ma], il collante [eel kol'lanteh]
hiking map of the area	mappa dei sentieri di questa zona [map'pa day sent-yairee dee kwesta dzona]
magazine	periodico [pairee-yodeeko]
map	carta geografica [karta jayografeeka]
newspaper	il giornale [eel jornaleh]
novel	romanzo [romand-zo]
pencil	matita [mateeta]
playing card	carta da gioco [karta da joko]
postcard	cartolina postale [kartoleena postaleh]
road map	carta stradale [karta stradaleh]
sketchbook	album da disegno [alboom da deesen-yo]
stamp	francobollo [frankobol'lo]
town map	pianta della città [pyanta del'la cheet'ta]
writing/letter paper	carta da lettere [karta da let'taireh]

 A ROOM WITH A VIEW

> A ROOM WITH A VIEW

Service with a smile: whether you want to pay a bill by credit card, access your hotel's Wi-Fi or get childcare at a holiday resort – all you have to do is ask!

GENERAL INFORMATION

> Planning Your Trip: page 6

Can you recommend..., please?	Scusi signora/signorina/signore, potrebbe consigliarmi …
	[skoozee seen-yora/seen-yoreena/seen-yoreh, potreb'beh konseel-yarmee]
a hotel, a guesthouse	un albergo/una pensione? [oon albairgo/oona pen-syoneh]
a campsite	un campeggio? [oon kampej'jo]
Can you recommend anywhere nearby?	Potrebbe consigliarmi qualcosa nei dintorni?
	[potreb'beh konseel-yarmee kwalkosa nay deentornee]

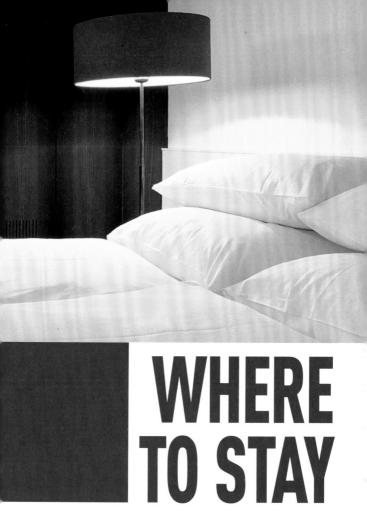

WHERE TO STAY

AT A HOTEL

I've reserved a room.	Ho prenotato una camera. [o prenotato oona kamaira]
My name is...	Il mio nome è … [eel mee-yo nomeh eh]
Have you got any vacancies?	Ha camere libere? [a kamaireh leebaireh]
...for one night.	… per una notte. [pair oona not'teh]
...for two days.	… per due giorni. [pair doo-eh jornee]
...for a week.	… per una settimana. [pair oona set'teemana]

No, sorry.	No, purtroppo no. [no, poortrop'po no]
Yes, what sort of room would you like?	Sì, che tipo di camera desidera? [see, keh teepo dee kamaira deseedaira]
a single room	una singola [oona seen-gola]
a double room	una matrimoniale [oona matreemon-yaleh]
with a shower	con doccia [kon dot'cha]
with a bathroom	con bagno [kon ban-yo]
a quiet room	una camera tranquilla [oona kamaira trankweel'la]
with a view of the sea	con vista sul mare [kon veesta sool mareh]
Can I see the room?	Posso vedere la camera? [pos'so vedaireh la kamaira]
Can you put another bed in the room?	Può aggiungere un altro letto? [pwo aj'joon-jaireh oon altro let'to]
Do you have Wi-Fi?	Avete Wi-Fi? [aveteh waee-faee]
How much is the room with...	Quanto costa la camera … [kwanto kosta la kamaira]
breakfast?	con la prima colazione? [kon la preema kolat-syoneh]
breakfast and an evening meal (half board)?	a mezza pensione? [a met'sa pen-syoneh]
full board?	a pensione completa? [a pen-syoneh kompleta]
What time is breakfast?	Da che ora si può fare colazione? [da keh ora see pwo fareh kolat-syoneh]
Where's the restaurant?	Dov'è il ristorante? [doveh eel reestoranteh]
Please wake me at... o'clock in the morning.	Mi svegli domattina alle …, per favore [mee zvel-yee domat'teena al'leh …, pair favoreh]
Can I have my key, please?	Per favore, la mia chiave. [pair favoreh, la mee-ya kyaveh]

> Breakfast: FOOD & DRINK, page 46

■COMPLAINTS | RECLAMI [reklamee]

The room hasn't been cleaned.	La camera non è stata pulita oggi. [la kamaira non eh stata pooleeta oj'jee]
The shower...	La doccia … [la dot'cha]
The toilet...	Lo sciacquone … [lo sh-yak'kwoneh]
The heating...	Il riscaldamento … [eel reeskaldamento]
The light...	La luce … [la loocheh]
...doesn't work.	non funziona. [non foont-syona]
There's no (warm) water.	Non c'è acqua (calda). [non cheh ak'kwa (kalda)]
The toilet/washbasin is blocked.	Il gabinetto/Il lavandino è intasato. [eel gabeenet'to/eel lavandeeno eh eentasato]

What time do I have to check out by?	Quando devo fare al mǫssimo il check out? [kwando devo fareh al mas'seemo eel chek-owt]
Can I leave my luggage/ baggage here till (this evening), please?	Posso lasciarli qui i bagagli fino a (stasera) [pos'so lasharlee kwee ee bagal-yee feeno a (stasaira)]
I'm leaving this evening/ tomorrow at... o'clock.	Parto stasera/domani alle … [parto stasaira/domanee al'leh]
Can I pay by credit card?	Accetta carte di crędito? [at'chet'ta karteh dee kredeeto]
Thank you very much for everything. Goodbye!	Grązie di tutto. Arrivederci! [grat-syeh dee toot'to ar'reevedairchee]

adapter	l'adattatore m [ladat'tatoreh]
air conditioning	aria condizionata [ar-ya kondeet-syonata]
baby monitor	il babyphone [eel baybee-fon]
babysitting service	baby-sitting m [baybee-seet'teeng]
bathrobe/dressing gown	l'accappatǫio [lak'kap'patoyo]
bathroom	bagno [ban-yo]
bed	letto [let'to]
bed and breakfast	pernottamento (con colazione) [pairnot'tamento (kon kolat-syoneh)]
bed linen	biancherįa da letto [byankairee-ya da let'to]
bedside table	comodino [komodeeno]
breakfast	la colazįone [la kolat-syoneh]
breakfast room	sala per la colazįone [sala pair la kolat-syoneh]
(chamber)maid	camerįera [kamair-yaira]
clean v	pulire [pooleereh]
cot	lettino (per bambįni) [let'teeno (pair bambeenee)]
cupboard	armądio [armad-yo]
dinner (evening meal)	cena [chena]
floor (storey)	piąno [pyano]
full board	la pensįone completa [la pen-syoneh kompleta]
half board	la mezzapensįone [la met'sa-pen-syoneh]
heating	riscaldamento [reeskaldamento]
high/low season	alta/bassa stagįone f [alta/bas'sa stajoneh]
iron n	il ferro da stiro [eel fair'ro da steero]
key	la chiąve [la kyaveh]
lamp	ląmpada [lampada]
lunch	pranzo [prand-zo], il desinare [eel dezeenareh]
pillow	cuscino [koosheeno]
playroom	la stanza giochi (per bambini) [la stant-sa jokee (pair bambeenee)]
plug	spina [speena]

porter	il portiere [eel port-yaireh]
reading lamp	lampada del comodino [lampada del komodeeno]
reception	l'accettazione [lat'chet'tat-syoneh], la reception [la ree-sep-syon]
reservation	la prenotazione [la prenotat-syoneh]
room	camera [kamaira]
safe	la cassaforte [la kas'saforteh]
shower	doccia [dot'cha]
socket (electric)	presa [presa]
tap/faucet	rubinetto [roobeenet'to]
toilet, toilet paper	gabinetto [gabeenet'to], carta igienica [karta eej-yeneeka]
towel	asciugamano [ashoogamano]
washbasin	lavandino [lavandeeno]
(cold/hot) water	acqua (fredda/calda) [ak'kwa (fred'da/kalda)]
window	finestra [feenestra]

LOCAL
KNOWLEDGE

Insider Tips

Your Dream Accommodation

Italy boasts accommodation for every taste and budget. Alongside all the usual hotels, apartments and guesthouses, you'll also find a couple of wonderful alternatives. Why not check out *caffelletto* [kaf'fel'let'to], for example, a wonderful selection of bed and breakfast-style accommodation located in old villas, medieval castles, and country estates. If you want a similar experience on a smaller budget, try out *agriturismo* [agreetooreezmo] ("farm holidays") for size. You'll find a wide selection of farms where you can stay the night – *aziende agrituristiche* [ad-zyendeh agreetooreesteekeh] – throughout the Italian peninsula. And if your budget allows, you could also enjoy waking up to the sound of the sea by renting chalets and apartments right on the beach.

> Whatever your preference, the MARCO POLO travel guides to Italy are a great way to help you make up your mind. You'll also get some great tips by visiting *www.marco-polo.com*.

Alberghi Diffusi

Alberghi diffusi [albairgee deef'foozee] ("scattered hotels") are a fantastic new concept for tourists. Found predominantly in the south of Italy away from the overcrowded tourist hotspots, these hotels are made up of rooms and apartments dotted around small villages. The (usually ensuite) accommodation – situated in restored villas, houses and farm buildings – is decorated in a way that reflects the tastes and styles of the region. A stay in these hotels allows you to feel part of local life without having to forgo the hotel comforts you love: you'll find a service centre with a central reception, restaurants, a swimming pool, a wellness spa and/or sporting facilities situated less than 200 metres from your accommodation. To find out more, visit: *www.alberghidiffusi.it*.

IN A HOLIDAY HOME

 Planning Your Trip: page 6

Is water/electricity included in the price?	La luce/L'acqua è compresa nel prezzo d'affitto? [la loocheh/lak'kwa eh kompresa nel pret'so daf'feet'to]
Are bed linen and towels provided?	Ci sono le lenzuola e gli asciugamani? [chee sono leh lent-swola eh l-yee ashoogamanee]
Where can we pick up the keys to the house/ the apartment?	Dove e quando posso ritirare le chiavi? [doveh eh kwando pos'so reeteerareh leh kyavee]
Do we have to clean the apartment before we leave?	Spetta a noi il lavoro di pulizia finale? [spet'ta a noy eel lavoro dee pooleet-see-ya feenaleh]

additional costs	le spese (accessorie) [leh speseh (at'ches'sor-yeh)]
bed linen	biancheria da letto [byankairee-ya da let'to]
bedroom	camera da letto [kamaira da let'to]
bottle opener	l'apribottiglie m [lapreebot'teel-yeh]
corkscrew	cavatappi m [kavatap'pee]
day of arrival	giorno d'arrivo [jorno dar'reevo]
deposit (down payment)	la caparra [la kapar'ra]
deposit (security)	la cauzione [la kowt-syoneh]
electricity	la corrente [la kor'renteh]
end-of-stay cleaning	pulizia finale [pooleet-see-ya feenaleh]
flat/apartment	appartamento [ap'partamento]
holiday camp	centro vacanze [chentro vakant-seh]
holiday flat/apartment	appartamento per le vacanze [ap'partamento pair leh vakant-seh]
holiday home	casa per le vacanze [kasa pair leh vakant-seh]
key	la chiave [la kyaveh]
kitchenette	cucinino [koocheeneeno], cucinotto [koocheenot'to]
landlord/lady	il padrone/la patrona di casa [eel padroneh/patrona dee kasa]
pets	gli animali domestici [l-yee aneemalee domesteechee]
rent n	affitto [af'feet'to], noleggio [nolej'jo]
rent v	affittare [af'feet'tareh], noleggiare [nolej'jareh]
rubbish/garbage	immondizia [eem'mondeet-sya]
sofa bed	divano letto [deevano let'to]
towel, dishcloth	asciugamano [ashoogamano], asciugapiatti [ashooga-pyat'tee]
waste sorting/separation	raccolta differenziata [rak'kolta deef'fairent-syata]

piatto
[pyat'to]

i bicchieri
[ee beek'kyairee]

tazza
[tat'sa]

portauovo
[porta-wovo]

forchetta
[forket'ta]

cucchiaio
[kook'kya-yo]

coltello
[koltel'lo]

cucchiaino
[kook'kya-yeeno]

mestolo
[mestolo]

la paletta da cucina
[la palet'ta da koocheena]

ramaiolo
[rama-yolo]

frusta
[froosta]

grattugia
[grat'tooja]

il tagliere
[eel tal-yaireh]

colino
[koleeno]

il frullatore
[eel frool'latoreh]

pentola
[pentola]

padella
[padel'la]

ciotola
[chotola]

cucina a gas
[koocheena a gas]

cucina economica/forno
[koocheena ekonomeeka/forno]

frigorifero
[freegoreefairo]

la lavastoviglie
[la lavastoveel-yeh]

la lavatrice
[la lavatreecheh]

il bollitore
[eel bol'leetoreh]

macchina del caffè
[mak'keena del kaf'feh]

filtro per il caffè
[feeltro pair eel kaf'feh]

il tostapane
[eel tostapaneh]

l'aspirapolvere m
[laspeerapolvaireh]

lavapavimento
[lavapaveemento]

ferro da stiro
[fair'ro da steero]

corda per stendere il bucato
[korda pair stendaireh eel bookato]

scopa
[skopa]

paletta per la spazzatura
[palet'ta pair la spat'satoora]

i prodotti per pulire
[ee prodot'tee pair pooleereh]

secchio
[sek'kyo]

AT A CAMPSITE

Have you got room for another caravan/tent?	C'è ancora posto per una roulotte/una tenda? [cheh ankora posto pair oona roolot/oona tenda]
How much does it cost per day and per person?	Quanto si paga al giorno a persona? [kwanto see paga al jorno a pairsona]
What's the price for...	Quanto si paga per ... [kwanto see paga pair]
the car?	l'auto? [lowto]
the caravan?	la roulotte? [la roolot]
the mobile home?	il camper? [eel kampair]
the tent?	la tenda? [la tenda]
We'll be staying for... days/weeks.	Rimaniamo ... giorni/settimane. [reeman-yamo ... jornee/set'teemaneh]
Is there a grocery store here?	C'è un negozio di alimentari? [cheh oon negot-syo dee aleementaree]
Where are...	Dove sono ... [doveh sono]
the toilets?	i servizi igienici? [ee sairveet-see eej-yen-eechee]
the washrooms?	i lavandini? [ee lavandeenee]
the showers?	le docce? [leh dot'cheh]
Are there any electric hook-up points here?	C'è una presa di corrente? [cheh oona presa dee kor'renteh]

advance reservation	preavviso [prayav'veezo]	
aluminium foil	foglio di alluminio [fol-yo dee al'loomeen-yo]	
barbeque/grill	griglia [greel-ya]	
bottle opener	l'apribottiglie m [lapreebot'teel-yeh]	
campervan/motorhome	il camper [eel kampair]	
camping	campeggiare [kampej'jareh]	
campsite	campeggio [kampej'jo]	
candles	le candele [leh kandeleh]	
caravan (Am: trailer)	la roulotte [la roolot]	
charcoal	carbonella [karbonel'la]	
cooker	fornello [fornel'lo]	
corkscrew	cavatappi m [kavatap'pee]	
cutlery	le posate [leh pozateh]	
drinking water	acqua potabile [ak'kwa potabeeleh]	
electric hook-up point	presa di corrente [presa dee kor'renteh]	
electricity	la corrente [la kor'renteh]	
gas bottle	bombola di gas [bombola dee gas]	
gas cooker	fornello a gas [fornel'lo a gas]	
hammer	il martello [eel martel'lo]	
hire	prestare [prestareh]	

hire charge	tariffa di noleggio [tareef'fa dee nolej'jo]
laundry pegs	molletta (per stendere la biancheria) [mol'let'ta (pair stendaireh la byankairee-ya)]
methylated spirits	spirito industriale [speereeto eendoostree-yaleh]
paraffin, paraffin lamp	petrolio [petrol-yo], lampada a petrolio [lampada a petrol-yo]
plug (electric)	spina [speena]
pocket knife	temperino [tempaireeno], coltello tascabile [koltel'lo taskabeeleh]
rubbish/garbage bags	sacco delle immondizie [sak'ko del'leh eem'mondeet-syeh]
service charge/utilisation fee	tassa per l'uso [tas'sa pair loozo]
sink	lavandino per i piatti [lavandeeno pair ee pyat'tee]
sleeping bag	il sacco a pelo [eel sak'ko a pelo]
socket (electric)	presa [presa]
spade	la vanga [la van-ga]
tent	tenda [tenda]
tent peg	il picchetto [eel peek'ket'to]
tent pole	palo da tenda [palo da tenda]
tin/can opener	l'apriscatole m [lapreeskatoleh]
torch/flashlight	la pila/torcia [la peela/torcha]
water	acqua [ak'kwa]

AT A YOUTH HOSTEL

Can I hire…?	Mi può prestare … [mee pwo prestareh]
…bedding	… la biancheria da letto? [la byankairee-ya da let'to]
…a sleeping bag	… un sacco a pelo [oon sak'ko a pelo]
The front door is locked at midnight.	Il portone d'ingresso viene chiuso alle ore 24. [eel portoneh deen-gres'so vee-yeneh kyooso al'leh oreh ventee-kwat'tro]

dormitory	dormitorio [dormeetor-yo]
kitchen	cucina [koocheena]
membership card	tessera di socio [tes'saira dee sochyo]
washroom	stanzino da bagno [stant-seeno da ban-yo]
Wi-Fi	Wi-Fi [waee-faee]
youth hostel	ostello della gioventù [ostel'lo del'la joventoo]
youth hostel card	tessera per gli ostelli della gioventù [tes'saira pair l-yee ostel'lee del'la joventoo]

> WHAT DO YOU WANT TO DO?

Whether you want an authentic cooking course, an exciting hiking trip or a great evening of theatre: the next few pages will help you experience loads of holiday adventures.

GENERAL INFORMATION

I'd like a map of...,
   please.
Vorrei una pianta di ... per favore.
   [vor'ray oona pyanta dee ... pair favoreh]

What tourist attractions are
   there here?
Che cosa c'è da vedere qui?
   [keh kosa cheh da vedaireh kwee]

Are there bus tours of
   the city?
Ci sono dei giri turistici della città?
   [chee sono day jeeree tooreesteechee del'la cheet'ta]

How much does the tour
   cost?
Quanto costa il biglietto?
   [kwanto kosta eel beel-yet'to]

A PACKED SCHEDULE

SIGHTSEEING/MUSEUMS

When is the museum open?	Quando è aperto il museo? [kwando eh apairto eel moozayo]
When does the tour start?	Quando comincia la visita guidata? [kwando komeencha la veezeeta gweedata]
Is there also a guided tour in English?	C'è una visita guidata anche in inglese? [cheh oona veezeeta gweedata ankeh een een-gleseh]
Is this/that...?	È questo il …/È questa la …? [eh kwesto eel …/eh kwesta la …]

altar	l'altare m [laltareh]
architecture	architettura [arkeetet'toora]
audio guide	audioguida [lowdee-yo-gweeda]
building	edificio [edeefeecho]
castle	castello [kastel'lo]
cathedral	la cattedrale [la kat'tedraleh], duomo [dwomo]
cemetery	cimitero [cheemeetairo]
century	secolo [sekolo]
chapel	cappella [kap'pel'la]
church	chiesa [kyeza]
day trip	gita di un giorno [jeeta dee oon jorno]
emperor, empress	l'imperatore m [leempairatoreh], l'imperatrice f [leempairatreecheh]
excavations	gli scavi [l-yee skavee]
exhibition	mostra [mostra], l'esposizione f [lespozeet-syoneh]
fortress	fortezza [fortet'sa]
(art) gallery	galleria (d'arte) [gal'lairee-ya [darteh]]
guide	guida turistica [gweeda tooreesteeka], il cicerone [eel cheechaironeh]
guided tour	visita guidata [veezeeta gweedata]
king, queen	re m [reh], regina [rejeena]
monument	monumento [monoomento]
museum	museo [moozayo]
painter	pittore [peet'toreh], pittrice [peet'treecheh]
painting	dipinto [deepeento]
palace	palazzo [palat'so]
picture	pittura [peet'toora]
religion	la religione [la releejoneh]
restore (refurbish)	restaurare [restowrareh]

A PACKED SCHEDULE

ruin n	rovina [roveena]
sculptor	lo scultore [lo skooltoreh]
sculpture	scultura [skooltoora]
service (relig.)	messa [mes'sa], la funzione sacra [la foont-syoneh sakra]
sights	le cose da vedersi [leh koseh da vedairsee], attrazioni [at'trat-syonee]
sightseeing tour of the town/city	giro della città [jeero del'la cheet'ta]
square	piazza [pyat'sa]
the old town	centro storico [chentro storeeko]
tour	visita [veezeeta]
tower	la torre [la tor'reh]
town hall, city hall	municipio [mooneecheepyo]

TRIPS & TOURS

What time are we meeting?	Quando ci incontriamo? [kwando chee eenkontree-yamo]
Where are we meeting?	Dov'è il punto d'incontro? [doveh eel poonto deenkontro]
Will we go past the...?	Passiamo da …? [pas'syamo da]
Are we going to see..., too?	Andiamo anche a vedere …? [and-yamo ankeh a vedaireh]
When are we coming back?	Quando torniamo? [kwando torn-yamo]

amusement park	parco divertimenti [parko deevairteementee]
botanical garden	giardino botanico [jardeeno botaneeko]
cave	grotta [grot'ta], caverna [kavairna]
countryside	paesaggio [pa-ezaj'jo]
(covered) market	mercato (coperto) [mairkato (kopairto)]
day trip	gita di un giorno [jeeta dee oon jorno]
fishing port/harbour	porto di pesca [porto dee peska]
fishing village	villaggio di pescatori [veel'laj'jo dee peskatoree]
forest	bosco [bosko]
game/wildlife park	riserva di caccia [reesairva dee kat'cha]
inland	entroterra [entrotair'ra]
island round-trip	giro dell'isola [jeero del'leezola]
lake	lago [lago]
mountain, mountain range	il monte [eel monteh], montagna [montan-ya]
mountain village	villaggio di montagna [veel'laj'jo dee montan-ya]
national park, nature reserve	parco nazionale [parko nat-syonaleh]
off-road vehicle	il fuoristrada [eel fworeestrada]
peak (mountain)	vetta [vet'ta], picco [peek'ko]
pilgrimage site	luogo di pellegrinaggio [lwogo dee pel'legreenaj'jo]
plantation	le piantagioni [leh pyantajonee]

ravine	gola [gola]
river	il fiume [eel fyoomeh]
sea	il mare [eel mareh]
spring (of water)	la sorgente [la sorjenteh], la fonte [la fonteh]
tour (round trip)	giro turistico [jeero tooreesteeko]
trip	gita [jeeta], l'escursione f [leskoor-syoneh]
vantage point	il belvedere [eel belvedaireh]
volcano	vulcano [voolkano]
waterfall	cascata [kaskata]
zoo	lo zoo [lo dzoh]

AFTER DARK

PUB/BAR/CLUB | PUB/BAR/CLUB [pab/bar/klab]

What's on...	Cosa c'è ...? [kosa cheh]
this weekend?	questo fine settimana? [kwesto feeneh set'teemana]
this evening?	stasera? [stasaira]
What is there to do here in the evenings?	Che cosa si puo' fare qui la sera? [keh kosa see pwo fareh kwee la saira]
Is there a nice pub here?	C'è un locale simpatico da queste parti? [cheh oon lokaleh seempateeko da kwesteh partee]
Where can we go dancing?	Dove si può andare a ballare? [doveh see pwo andareh a bal'lareh]
What kind of music do they play here?	Che tipo di musica suonano qui? [keh teepo dee moozeeka swonano kwee]
A whisky and soda, please.	Un whisky e soda, per favore. [oon weeskee eh soda, pair favoreh]
The same again, please.	Un'altro/Un altra, per favore. [oon-altro/oon altra, pair favoreh]
This round's on me.	Stavolta offro io. [stavolta of'fro ee-yo]
Shall we dance?	Balliamo? [bal'l-yamo]
band	complesso [komples'so]
bar, club, disco	il bar [eel bar], il club [eel klab], discoteca [deeskoteka]
bouncer	il portiere [eel portee-yaireh]
dance v	ballare [bal'lareh]
folk music	musica folk [moozeeka folk]
gay/lesbian scene	la comunità gay/lesbica [la komooneeta gay/lezbeeka]
go out	uscire [oosheereh]
live music	musica dal vivo [moozeeka dal veevo]
party	party m [partee]
pub/bar	osteria [ostairee-ya], il pub [eel pab]

A PACKED SCHEDULE

THEATRE/CONCERT/CINEMA
TEATRO/CONCERTO/CINEMA [teatro/konchairto/cheenema]

Have you got a diary of events for this week?	Ha un programma delle manifestazioni di questa settimana? [a oon program'ma del'leh maneefestat-syonee dee kwesta set'teemana]
What's on at the theatre tonight?	Scusi, saprebbe dirmi che pezzo danno oggi a teatro? [skoozee, sapreb'beh deermee keh pet'so dan'no oj'jee a tayatro]
Can you recommend a good play?	Mi può consigliare una buona rappresentazione teatrale? [mee pwo konseel-yareh oona bwona rap'prezentat-syoneh tayatraleh]
When does the performance start?	Quando comincia lo spettacolo? [kwando komeencha lo spet'takolo]
Where can I get tickets?	Dove si comprano i biglietti? [doveh see komprano ee beel-yet'tee]
(Two) tickets for this evening, please.	(Due) biglietti per stasera, per favore. [(doo-eh) beel-yet'tee pair stasaira, pair favoreh]
A programme/playbill, please.	Mi può dare un programma, per favore? [mee pwo dareh oon program'ma, pair favoreh]
Where's the cloakroom?	Dov'è il guardaroba? [doveh eel gwardaroba]

audio guide	l'audioguida [lowdee-yo-gweeda]
advance booking	prevendita [prevendeeta]
ballet	balletto [bal'let'to]
box office	cassa [kas'sa]
calendar of events	calendario delle manifestazioni [kalendar-yo del'leh maneefestat-syonee]
cinema, film/movie	il cinema [eel cheenema], il film [eel feelm]
concert	concerto [konchairto]
performance/screening	spettacolo [spet'takolo]
premiere	prima [preema]
theatre	teatro [tayatro]
ticket	biglietto [beel-yet'to]

LOCAL KNOWLEDGE

Insider Tip

Never Overdressed

While in Italy, it's well worth taking a trip to one of the old-style Italian theatres. They usually put on a fantastic variety of shows, ranging from plays, ballets and operas, right through to jazz and pop concerts.

Make sure to dress for the occasion in the more venerable establishments. Elegance is key here – the word 'overdressed' does not appear in the Italian vocabulary!

Could you tell me when the... festival takes place, please?	Scusi, potrebbe dirmi quando avrà luogo il Festival ...? [skoozee, potreb'beh deermee kwando avra lwogo eel festeeval]
from... to.../every (2) years	dal ... al .../ogni (due) anni [dal ... al/on-yee (doo-eh) an'nee]
every year in August	ogni anno in agosto [on-yee an'no een agosto]

carnival	carnevale m [karnevaleh]
fair/fête/street party	sagra [sagra]
festival	il fęstival [eel festeeval]
fireworks	fuochi artificiali [fwokee arteefeechalee]
flea market	mercatino delle pulci [mairkateeno del'leh poolchee]
funfair	fiera [fyaira]
Mardi Gras, Shrove Tuesday	martedì grasso [martedee gras'so]
May Day	Calendimąggio [kalendeemaj'jo]
parade, procession	processione [proches'syoneh], sfilata [sfeelata]
village fête	festa del paese [festa del pa-yezeh]

AT THE BEACH & SPORTS

Is there a strong current?	È molto forte la corrente? [eh molto forteh la kor'renteh]
Is it dangerous for children?	È pericoloso per i bambini? [eh paireekoloso pair ee bambeenee]
When's low tide/high tide?	Quando vięne la bassa maręa/l'alta maręa? [kwando vee-yeneh la bas'sa maraya/lalta maraya]

(swimming) beach	spiąggia (balenabile) [sp-yaj'ja (balenabeeleh)]
changing rooms	cabine f, pl [kabeeneh]
current	la corrente [la kor'renteh]
jellyfish	medusa [medooza]
kiosk	(for newspapers) edįcola [edeekola], (general sales) chiosco [kyosko]
lifeguard	bagnino [ban-yeeno]
nudist beach	spiąggia per nudisti [sp-yaj'ja pair noodeestee]
sand	sabbia [sab'bya]
shower	dǫccia [dot'cha]
sunshade/parasol	l'ombrellone m [lombrel'loneh]
swim v	nuotare [nwotareh]

A PACKED SCHEDULE

ACTIVE HOLIDAYS/SPORT
VACANZE ATTIVE/SPORT [vakant-seh at-teeveh/sport]

What sports facilities are there here?	Quali sport si possono praticare qui? [kwalee sport see pos'sono prateekareh kwee]
Is there a... here?	C'è un/una ... qui? [cheh oon/oona ... kwee]
Where can I hire...?	Dove posso noleggiare ...? [doveh pos'so nolej'jareh]
I'd like to take a... course for beginners/ an advanced... course.	Vorrei fare un corso di ... per principianti/avanzati. [vor'ray fareh oon korso dee pair preencheepyantee/avant-satee]

contest/match	gara [gara]
defeat n	sconfitta [skonfeet'ta]
draw/tie n	pari m [paree]
lose v	perdere [pairdaireh]
match/game	partita [parteeta]
race	corsa [korsa]
referee/umpire	arbitro [arbeetro]
team/crew	squadra [skwadra]
victory/win n	vittoria [veet'tor-ya]
win v	vincere [veenchaireh]

WATER SPORTS SPORT ACQUATICO [sport ak'kwateeko]

boat hire	noleggio di barche [nolej'jo dee barkeh]
boating licence/permit	la patente nautica [la patenteh nowteeka]
canoe	canoa [kano-a]
houseboat	la house boat [la owss boht]
indoor pool	piscina coperta [peesheena kopairta]
inflatable/rubber dinghy/boat	canotto pneumatico [kanot'to pnayoomateeko]
motorboat	motoscafo [motoskafo]
open air pool	piscina all'aperto [peesheena al'tapairto]
pedalo/pedal boat	pattino a pedali [pat'teeno a pedalee]
pick-up service	servizio rimpatrio [sairveet-syo reempatree-yo]
rowing boat	barca a remi [barka a remee]
sailing	vela [vela], veleggiata [velej'jata], gita in barca a vela [jeeta een barka a vela]
sailing boat	barca a vela [barka a vela]
sailing school	scuola vela [skwola vela]
surf school	scuola surf [skwola surf]
surfboard	tavoletta per il surf [tavolet'ta pair eel surf]
surfing	praticare il surfing [prateekareh eel surfeeng]
water skiing	gli sci nautici [l-yee shee nowteechee]
windsurfing	il windsurf [eel weendsurf], fare windsurf [fareh weendsurf]

DIVING NUOTARE SOTT'ACQUA [nwotareh sot'tak'kwa]

breathing/oxygen apparatus	l'ossigenatore m [los'seejenatoreh]
dive v	nuotare sott'acqua [nwotareh sot'tak'kwa]
diving equipment	attrezzatura da palombaro [at'tret'satoora da palombaro]
diving mask	gli occhiali da immersione [l-yee ok'kyalee da eem'mair-syoneh]
diving school	scuola immersione [skwola eem'mair-syoneh]
flippers	le pinne [leh peen'neh]
go snorkelling	fare lo snorkeling [fareh lo znorkeleeng]
harpoon	fiocina [fyo-cheena]
scuba diving	immersione con le bombole [eem'mair-syoneh kon leh bomboleh]
snorkel	il respiratore di superficie [eel respeeratoreh dee soopairfeech-yeh]
wetsuit	la muta in neoprene [la moota een nayopreneh]

FISHING PESCA [peska]

Where can I go fishing?	Dove si può pescare? [doveh see pwo peskareh]
bait	esca [eska]
deep-sea fishing	pesca d'alto mare [peska dalto mareh]
fishing licence	licenza di pesca [leechent-sa dee peska]
fishing rod	pescare [peskareh]
go fishing	pesca [peska]
off/close season	periodo di divieto di caccia [pairee-yodo dee deev-yeto dee kat'cha]

BALL GAMES GIOCHI A PALLA [jokee a pal'la]

ball	palla [pal'la], pallone m [pal'loneh]
basketball	il basket [eel basket], la pallacanestro [pal'lakanestro]
football	calcio [kalchyo]
football ground	campo da gioco (del calcio) [kampo da joko (del kalchyo)]
football team	squadra di calcio [skwadra dee kalchyo]
goal	porta [porta], il goal [eel gol]
goalkeeper	il portiere [eel port-yaireh]
net	la rete [la reteh]
volleyball	la pallavolo [la pal'lavolo]

TENNIS, ETC. TENNIS E SIMILI [ten'nees eh seemeelee]

badminton	il badminton [eel badmeenton], gioco del volano [joko del volano]
covered (tennis) court	campo (da tennis) coperto [kampo (da ten'nees) kopairto]
racket/racquet	racchetta [rak'ket'ta]
squash	lo squash [lo skwash]
table tennis	il ping-pong [eel peeng-pong]
tennis, tennis court	il tennis [eel ten'nees], campo da tennis [kampo da ten'nees]
tennis racket/racquet	racchetta [rak'ket'ta]

A PACKED SCHEDULE

FITNESS & WEIGHT TRAINING FITNESS E POWER TRAINING [feetnes eh powair traineeng]

aerobics	aerobica [a-yairobeeka]
fitness centre	centro ginnico [chentro jeen'neeko]
fitness training	allenamento per migliorare la forma
	[al'lenamento pair meel-yorareh la forma]
go jogging/jog v	fare jogging m [fareh jog'geeng]
weight training	allenamento con i pesi [al'lenamento kon ee pesee]
yoga, Pilates	lo yoga [lo yoga], il pilates [leel peelates]

WELLBEING BENESSERE [benes'saireh]

acupressure	l'acupressura [lakoopres'soora]
aromatherapy	l'aromoterapia [laromotairapee-ya]
baths/bathhouse	i bagni [ee ban-yee]
beauty treatment	il trattamento beauty [eel trat'tamento byootee]
diet foods	l'alimentazione dietetica [laleementat-syoneh dee-yeteteeka]
hammam, Turkish bath	l'hammam m [lam'mam], bagno turco [ban-yo toorko]
manicure, pedicure	la manicura [la maneekoora], la pedicura [la pedeekoora]
massage	massaggio [mas'saj'jo]
skin peeling treatment	il peeling [eel peeleeng]
solarium	solario [solar-yo]

CYCLING CICLISMO [cheekleezmo]

bicycle/bike	bicicletta [beecheeklet'ta]
crash helmet	casco di protezione [kasko dee protet-syoneh]
cycle path	pista ciclabile [peesta cheeklabeeleh], ciclopista [cheeklopeesta]
cycle race	corsa ciclistica [korsa cheekleesteeka]
cycle tour	gita in bicicletta [jeeta een beecheeklet'ta]
cycle v	andare in bicicletta [andareh een beecheeklet'ta]
electric bike	l'e-bike f [lee-ba-eek]
(inner) tube	camera d'aria [kamaira dar-ya]
mountain bike	la mountain bike [la mownten ba-eek]
pump	pompa d'aria [pompa dar-ya]
(puncture) repair kit	gli accessori per la riparazione di forature
	[l-yee at'ches'soree pair la reeparat-syoneh dee foratooreh]
racing bike	bicicletta da corsa [beecheeklet'ta da korsa]

HIKING & MOUNTAINEERING TREKKING E ALPINISMO [trek'keeng eh alpeeneezmo]

I'd like to go for a hike in the mountains.	Vorrei fare una gita in montagna.
	[vor'ray fareh oona jeeta een montan-ya]
Can you show me an interesting route on the map?	Mi può indicare un itinerario interessante sulla carta?
	[mee pwo eendeekareh oon eeteen-air-ar-yo eentaires'santeh sool'la karta]
cable car/funicular railway	funivia [fooneevee-ya], la funicolare [la fooneekolareh]
day trip/excursion	marcia di un giorno [marcha dee oon jorno]

hiking	camminare [kam'meenareh]
hiking map	mappa dei sentieri [map'pa day sent-yairee]
long-distance hiking route	sentiero per escursioni a lunga distanza
	[sent-yairo pair eskoorsyonee a loon-ga deestant-sa]
mountaineering	alpinismo [alpeeneezmo]
mountain guide	guida alpina [gweeda alpeena]
path	sentiero per escursioni [sent-yairo pair eskoors-yonee]
route	percorso [pairkorso], itinerario [eeteen-air-ar-yo]
safety rope	corda di sicurezza [korda dee seekooret'sa]

RIDING CAVALCARE [kavalkareh]

equestrian holidays	le vacanze a cavallo [leh vakant-seh a kaval'lo]
equestrianism/	l'equitazione f [lekweetat-syoneh], ippica [eep'peeka]
equestrian sports	
horse	cavallo [kaval'lo]
ride n, ride v/go riding	cavalcata [kavalkata], cavalcare [kavalkareh]
riding school	scuola di equitazione [skwola dee ekweetat-syoneh]

GOLF IL GOLF [eel golf]

golf club	mazza da golf [mat'sa da golf]
golf course	campo da golf [kampo da golf]
green fee	il greenfee [eel greenfee]
a round of golf	giocare una partita a golf [jokareh oona parteeta a golf]
visitor	il visitatore giornaliero [eel veezeetatoreh jornal-yairo]

IN THE AIR ALL'ARIA APERTA [al'lar-ya apairta]

gliding	volo a vela [volo a vela]
hang gliding	lo sport del deltaplano
	[lo sport del deltaplano]
parachuting	paracadutismo [parakadooteezmo]
paragliding	il parapendio [eel parapendee-yo]
parasailing	parapendio a motore trainante
	[parapendee-yo a motoreh traeenanteh]

WINTER HOLIDAYS VACANZE INVERNALI [vakant-seh eenvairnalee]

A day ticket, please.	Un (biglietto) giornaliero, per favore.
	[oon (beel-yet'to) jornal-yairo, pair favoreh]
What time is the last trip	A che ora c'è l'ultima salita a monte/discesa a valle?
up the mountain/	[a keh ora cheh loolteema saleeta a monteh/deeshesa a val'leh]
down into the valley?	

binding	attacco [at'tak'ko]
bottom/top ski lift station	la stazione a valle/monte [la stat-syoneh a val'leh/monteh]
cable car	cabina [kabeena]

A PACKED SCHEDULE

cross-country ski course	pista di fondo [peesta dee fondo]
cross-country skiing	lo sci di fondo [lo shee dee fondo]
day pass	(abbonamento) giornaliero [[ab'bonamento] jornal-yairo]
(ice) hockey	l'hockey m (su ghiaccio) [lok'key [soo gyat'chyo]]
ice rink	pista per pattinaggio su ghiaccio [peesta pair pat'teenaj'jo soo gyat'chyo]
ice skates	i pattini (per ghiaccio) [ee pat'teenee (pair gyat'chyo]]
ice skating	pattinaggio su ghiaccio [pat'teenaj'jo soo gyat'chyo]
ski n, ski v/go skiing	lo sci [lo shee], sciare [sh-yareh]
ski goggles	gli occhiali da sci [l-yee ok'kyalee da shee]
ski instructor	maestro m/maestra f di sci [ma-estro/ma-estra dee shee]
ski lift	lo sciovia [lo shyo-vee-ya], lo ski-lift [lo skee-lift]
ski poles	i bastoni da sci [ee bastonee da shee]
skiing lessons	corso di sci [korso dee shee]
snowboard n, toboggan	lo snowboard [lo znowboard], slitta [zleet'ta]
week pass	abbonamento settimanale [ab'bonamento set'teemanaleh]

COURSES

I would like to take an Italian language course	Mi interesserebbe fare un corso d'italiano. [mee eentaires'sair-eb'beh fareh oon korso deetal-yano]
for beginners.	per principianti [pair preencheepyantee]
for advanced learners.	per avanzati [pair avant-satee]
Is prior knowledge required?	Sono richieste delle conoscenze preliminari? [sono reekyesteh del'leh konoshent-seh preleemeenaree]
Are materials included in the price?	I costi per il materiale sono compresi? [ee kostee pair eel matair-yaleh sono kompresee]
What should I bring along?	Cosa si deve portare? [kosa see deveh portareh]

belly dancing	danza del ventre [dant-sa del ventreh]
carpentry workshop	i lavori di falegnameria [ee lavoree dee falen-yamairee-ya]
cooking	il cucinare [eel koocheenareh], la cucina [la koocheena]
course	corso [korso]
drumming	il suonare/battere il tamburo [eel swonareh/bat'taireh eel tambooro]
goldsmithery	i lavori d'oreficeria [ee lavoree dore-feech-yairee-ya]
life drawing	disegno di nudi [deesen-yo dee noodee]
oil/watercolour painting	pittura a olio/di acquerello [peet'toora a ol-yo/dee ak'kwairel'lo]
photography	fotografare [fotografareh]
workshop (class)	il workshop [eel workshop]

I'm stuffed/full

(lit: I'm as full as an egg)

Sono pieno come un uovo
[sono pyeno komeh oon wovo]

> WORDS GONE WILD

When your dictionary fails you and everyone seems to be talking gobbledegook, you've most likely been plunged headfirst into the wonderful world of slang.

BECOME **AN INSIDER**

Who hasn't been in this situation: you've made some contacts in a foreign land and are excitedly listening to your new friends chatting away – but their speech is littered with mysterious words that quite simply leave you in the dark. That's because there's a world of difference between the language you'll find in the dictionary and the language people actually use on the street. But don't panic: over the next few pages, we'll plunge you headfirst into the lingo that's spoken in cafés, clubs, bars, shops, hotels and hostels, and show you the way people talk when they're chatting on the bus, on the train, and in the lively

WARNING! SLANG

squares of villages, towns and cities. We've tracked down all the most authentic, essential and downright funniest slang expressions to give you some all-important insider knowledge. But beware: there are some phrases that are better left unsaid! Also, bear in mind that slang is often a very local affair and that pronunciation can vary from region to region. But with a bit of patience, you'll be able to get a handle on all the different regional dialects and listen in on what everyone has to say.

Have fun reading this chapter and broadening your vocabulary!

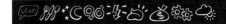

DAY TO DAY

blah

GREETINGS, ETC.

Ciao a tutti! [chow a toot'tee]	Hi everyone!
Ciao caro/cara! [chow karo/kara]	Hi darling/babe! (man/woman)
Chi non muore si rivede! [kee non mworeh see reevedeh]	Long time, no see!
Stammi bene! [stam'mee beneh]	Take care of yourself!
In bocca al lupo!/In culo alla balena!	Good luck!/Break a leg! (lit: in the
[een bok'ka al loopo/een koolo al'la balena]	wolf's mouth/in the whale's arse/ass)
Ci sentiamo. [chee sent-yamo]	Talk to you soon./We'll talk soon.

RESPONSES

Me ne frego. [meh neh frego]	I don't give a damn.
Non me ne frega un cazzo. [non meh neh frega oon kat'so]	I really don't care. (cazzo = lit: dick/prick)
Che ne so? [keh neh so]	How should I know?
Non capisco un cazzo. [non kapeesko oon kat'so]	It's all Greek to me.
Che cavolo/cazzo vuoi? [keh kavolo/kat'so vwoy]	What the hell do you want?
	(cavolo = lit: cabbage)
Che cavolo/cazzo te ne frega?	What the hell's it to you?/What the
[keh kavolo/kat'so teh neh frega]	hell's it got to do with you?
Col cazzo che lo faccio! [kol kat'so keh lo fat'ch-yo]	I'll be damned if I will!
Non ci penso neanche! [non chee penso nay-ankeh]	I wouldn't dream of it!
Neanche per sogno! [nay-ankeh pair son-yo]	No way! (lit: not even in a dream)

COMMANDS

Senti un po'... [sentee oon po]	Listen.../Listen up...
Datti una mossa! [dat'tee oona mos'sa]	Move your arse!/Shift your ass!
Non te la prendere! [non teh la prendaireh]	Don't worry!/Don't sweat it!
Camomillati! [kamomeel'latee]	Calm down!
Datti una calmata! [dat'tee oona kalmata]	Keep calm!/Keep your hair on!

AMONG FRIENDS...

dare un colpo di telefono [dareh oon kolpo dee telefono]	to give someone a ring
messaggiare [mes'saj'jareh]	to send an SMS/a text message
darsi una punta/un puntello	to make a date/arrange to meet
[darsee oona poonta/oon poontel'lo]	

WARNING! SLANG

fare un giro con qc [fareh oon jeero kon kwalkoono] — to hang out with someone
fare lo struscio/fare le vasche — to stroll/walk around (in the evening = meet at the piazza)
[fareh lo stroosh-yo/fareh leh vaskeh]
bazzicare [bat'seekareh] — to hang around with someone
fare quattro chiacchiere [fareh kwat'tro kyak'kyaireh] — to chat
ghignare [geen-yareh] — to laugh
farsela addosso [farsela ad'dos'so] — to laugh yourself silly
dirlo chiaro e tondo [deerlo kyaro eh tondo] — to say it straight/clearly
Ha il pelo sullo stomaco. [a eel pelo sool'lo stomako] — He's/She's tough.
  (lit: he/she has hair on his/her stomach)*

Fa il figo. [fa eel feego] — He's/She's so vain/smug/bigheaded.
menarsela/tirarsela [menarsela/teerarsela] — to show off/be full of oneself
Ha la faccia tosta. [a la fat'cha tosta] — He's/She's got cheek.
spararle grosse/raccontarla grossa — to lie through one's teeth
[spararleh gros'seh/rak'kontarla gros'sa]
sgamare [zgamareh] — to rumble (someone)
fare una figuraccia [fareh oona feegoorat'cha] — make a fool of yourself
un guastafeste [oon gwasta-festeh] — a party pooper

■THAT'S GREAT...

Un delirio! [oon deleer-yo] — Wicked!
Che sballo! [keh zbal'lo] — Awesome!
È una bomba! [eh oona bomba] — That's amazing!
Alla grande! [al'la grandeh] — That's fantastic!/That rocks!
È partito! [eh parteeto] — It's wicked!
È una bazza. [eh oona bat'sa] — It's gorgeous.
Che forza! [keh fort-sa] — Cool!
Mi piace una cifra. [mee pee-yacheh oona cheefra] — I think that's brilliant.
Che figata! [keh feegata] — Brilliant!
È fuori di testa. [eh fworee dee testa] — He's/She's over the moon.
Ci va grassa! [chee va gras'sa] — We're feeling/doing fantastic!
Che culo! [keh koolo] — How lucky!/What luck!

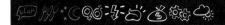

THAT'S BORING...

Uffa! [oof'fa] — Oh no!
Che barba! [keh barba] — How boring! (lit: what a beard!)
palloso [pal'loso] — boring
annoiarsi a morte [an'noyarsee a morteh] — to be bored to death

THAT'S ANNOYING

dare i nervi [dareh ee nairvee] — to get on (someone's) nerves
Che palle! [keh pal'leh] — That sucks!/That's annoying!
uno sbatti/sbattimento [oono zbat'tee/zbat'teemento] — an annoying situation
cazzate/vaccate [kat'sateh/vak'kateh] — bullshit
un mucchio di stronzate [oon mook'kyo dee stront-sateh] — absolute rubbish/bullshit
rompere i coglioni/le palle a qc — to get on someone's nerves
  [rompaireh ee kol-yonee/leh pal'leh a kwalkoono]
È una fregatura. [eh oona fregatoora] — What a bummer/wash-out.

FEELING BAD?

Non sono in forma. [non sono een forma] — I'm feeling under the weather.
Non sono in vena. [non sono een vena] — I don't feel good.
È nel pallone. [eh nel pal'loneh] — He's/She's confused.
scoglionato [skol-yonato] — annoyed/pissed off
Che casino/bordello! [keh kaseeno/bordel'lo] — What a shambles!/What carnage!
Sono incasinato. [sono eenkaseenato] — I'm in a mess.
Ha la luna storta. [a la loona storta] — He's/She's in a bad mood.
  (lit: he has a crooked moon)

essere giù [es'saireh joo] — to be low/cut up/down
prendersela [prendairsela] — to be offended/insulted
scoglionarsi [skol-yonarsee] — to get angry, annoyed/
   to not be arsed/assed

Mi sono rotto (le palle)./Ne ho le palle piene. — I'm fed up.
  [mee sono rot'to (leh pal'leh)/neh o leh pal'leh pyeneh]

Ristorante

*

WARNING! SLANG

Sono stufo/a! [sono stoofo/a]
I'm fed up with it/sick of it!

incavolato/incazzato [eenkavolato/eenkat'sato]
annoyed/pissed off

Mi fa schifo! [mee fa skeefo]
It makes me want to puke!

essere a terra [es'saireh a tair'ra]
to be devastated

essere alla frutta [es'saireh al'la froot'ta]
to be at rock bottom
(lit: to be at the fruit [dessert])

Che sfiga! [keh sfeega]
What bad luck!

uno sfigato [oono sfeegato]
an unlucky person/a loser

avere la tremarella [avaireh la tremarel'la]
to be scared stiff

farsela addosso/farsela sotto/cagarsi sotto
[farsela ad'dos'so/farsela sot'to/kagarsee sot'to]
to shit your pants with fear

prendersela nel culo/in quel posto
[prendairsela nel koolo/een kwel posto]
to be taken for a ride

perdere la testa [pairdaireh la testa]
to freak out

FOOD

Sto morendo di fame! [sto morendo dee fameh]
I'm dying of hunger!

Fa venire l'acquolina in bocca.
[fa veneereh lak'kwoleena een bok'ka]
My mouth is watering.

mangiare un boccone/fare uno spuntino
[manjareh oon bok'koneh/fareh oono spoon-teeno]
to have a snack

mangiare in bianco [manjareh een byanko]
to eat plain/simple food

farsi due spaghetti [farsee doo-eh spaget'tee]
to make some (lit: two strands of) pasta

con un filo/filino d'olio [kon oon feelo/feeleeno dol-yo]
with a very small amount of oil

fare la scarpetta [fareh la skarpet'ta]
to mop sauce from your plate with some bread (lit: do the little shoe)*

sbafarsi un panino [zbafarsee oon paneeno]
to scoff/scarf down a sandwich

fare una scorpacciata/un'abbuffata [fareh oona skorpat'chata/oon-ab'boof'fata]
to stuff yourself

Sono pieno come un uovo. [sono pyeno komeh oon wovo]
I'm stuffed/full. (lit: I'm as full as an egg)

Non sa di niente. [non sa dee nyenteh]
It doesn't taste of anything.

Fa schifo. [fa skeefo]
It tastes disgusting.

GOING OUT

■DRINKS■

Salute!/Cin cin! [salooteh/cheen cheen]
Cheers!/To your health!

un drink [oon dreenk]
an alcoholic drink

uno spritz/una bicicletta
[oono spreets/oona beecheeklet'ta]
un bombardino [oon bombardeeno]

acquavitaccia [ak'kwaveet-at'cha]

north Italian aperitif made from
white wine
alcoholic drink
(served hot at ski resorts)
booze, hooch

AT THE BAR/PUB

farsi una bevuta con gli amici
[farsee oona bevoota kon l-yee ameechee]
fare un brindisi [fareh oon breendeesee]
alzare il gomito [alt-sareh eel gomeeto]
tazzare [tat'sareh]
sbronzarsi/prendersi una sbornia
[zbront-sarsee/prendairsee oona zborn-ya]
tirare tardi [teerareh tardee]
fare le ore piccole
[fareh leh oreh peek'koleh]
il buttafuori [eel boot'ta-fworee]
musica da sballo [moozeeka da zbal'lo]
strapieno/murato [strap-yeno/moorato]
tirato/a [teerato/a]

to go for a drink with friends

to drink a toast/raise a glass
to have a drink (lit: lift an elbow)
to booze/have a few
to get drunk/hammered

to stay out late
to the pull an all-nighter
(lit: to do the small hours)
bouncer
awesome music
packed/chock-full
dressed up/tarted up/decked-out

LATER ON...

brillo [breel'lo]
Sono sfatto/fuso. [sono sfat'to/foozo]
sbronzo [zbront-so]
ubriaco fradicio [oobree-yako fradeech-yo]
È fuori come un balcone.
[eh fworee komeh oon balkoneh]

tipsy
I'm dog tired.
drunk/wasted
blind drunk
He's/She's roaring/dead drunk.
(lit: he is outside like a balcony)

SMOKING

il tabacchino [eel tabak'keeno]
una paglia [oona pal-ya]
una cicca [oona cheek'ka]
stabaccare [stabak'kareh]
fumare come un turco
[foomareh komeh oon toorko]
un fumatore incallito [oon foomatoreh eenkal'leeto]

tabacconist
cigarette
a smoke/a ciggy/a cigarette
to puff away
to smoke like a chimney
(lit: to smoke like a Turkish person)
a chain smoker

WARNING! SLANG

MEN & WOMEN

■ PEOPLE

un tipo/un tizio [oon teepo/oon teet-syo]	guy/dude
una tipa/una tizia [oona teepa/oona teet-sya]	girl/chick
un/a fuoriclasse [oon(a) fworeeklas'seh]	a fantastic guy/girl
un tipo sgamato [oon teepo zgamato]	a cool guy
un figo [oon feego]	a cool dude
una gran figa [oona gran feega]	a hot woman
È ben dotato. [eh ben dotato]	He's well hung.
una tettona [oona tet'tona]	a woman with large breasts
Ha un bel davanzale. [a oon bel davant-saleh]	She's well endowed/has a large rack.
	(lit: she has a beautiful windowsill)*
un cocco di mamma [oon kok'ko dee mam'ma]	a mummy's boy
una stangona [oona stan-gona]	a beanpole

■ FLIRTING & MORE...

Mi piace un sacco/un casino.	I'm totally in to him/her.
[mee pee-yacheh oon sak'ko/oon kaseeno]	
Complimenti alla mamma!	You look amazing!
[kompleementee al'la mam'ma]	
È uno schianto! [eh oono sk-yanto]	She's a knockout!
lumare [loomareh]	to stare/ogle
abbordare/intortare [ab'bordareh/eentortareh]	to chat up/hit on someone
flirtare [fleertareh]	to flirt
È cotto di lei.	He's got a crush on her.
[eh kot'to dee lay]	(lit: he's being cooked by her)
pomiciare [pomeechareh]	to make out
farsela con qc [farsela kon kwalkoono]	to have a fling with someone
cuccare [kook'kareh], rimorchiare [reemork-yareh]	to pick (someone) up
avercelo duro [avairchelo dooro]	to have an erection
il goldone [eel goldoneh]	condom

*

fare una scopata/scopare [fareh oona skopata/skopareh]	to have sex (lit: to sweep)*
una sveltina [oona zvelteena]	a quickie
dare un bidone/tirare un pacco a qc	to stand someone up
[dareh oon beedoneh/teerareh oon pak'ko a kwalkoono]	
piantare/mollare/lasciare qc	to break up with someone
[pyantareh/mol'lareh/lash-yareh kwalkoono]	
Lo ha scaricato. [lo a skareekato]	He's/she's dumped him/her.
Una lasciata, cento di trovate.	There are plenty more fish in the sea.
[oona lash-yata, chento dee trovateh]	(lit: let one go, found a hundred)
un matrimonio riparatore [oon matreemon-yo reeparatoreh]	a shotgun wedding
l'addio al celibato [lad'dyo al cheleebato]	Stag/Hen party, Bachelor/ette party
In casa loro è lei che porta i pantaloni.	She wears the trousers/pants in that
[een kasa loro eh lay keh porta ee pantalonee]	house.

RANTING, BITCHING, SWEARING

⚡

THE BASICS

Mamma mia!/Dio mio! [mam'ma mee-ya/dee-yo mee-yo]	Oh my gosh!/Oh my god!
Per carità! [pair kareeta]	For heaven's sake!
Cavolo! [kavolo]	Damn!/Kudos! (lit: cabbage)
Porca miseria/puttana! [porka meezair-ya/poot'tana]	Damn!/Hell!
Merda! [mairda]	Shit!
Maledizione! [maledeet-syoneh]	Damn!/Shoot!/Hell's bells!
Chiudi il becco! [kyoodee eel bek'ko]	Shut your face!
Non rompere (le palle/i coglioni!)	Don't annoy me!
[non rompaireh (leh pal'leh/ee kol-yo-nee)]	
Levati dai piedi! [levatee daee pyedee]	Beat it!/Piss off!
Levati dalle palle/dai coglioni!	Get the hell out of here!
[levatee dal'leh pal'leh/daee kol-yonee]	(palle/coglioni = lit: balls/testicles)
Vaffanculo!/Vai a farti fottere!	Piss off!/Get lost!
[vaf'fankoolo/vaee a fartee fot'taireh]	
Scordatelo! [skordatelo]	Bite me!/Sod off!
Cavoli/Cazzi tuoi! [kavolee/kat'see twoy]	Tough shit!/Tough titty!
inculare qc [eenkoolareh kwalkoono]	to pull a fast one on someone
sfottere/prendere per il culo	to bust someone's balls/
[sfot'taireh/prendaireh pair eel koolo]	take the piss out of someone
sputtanare qc [spoot'tanareh kwalkoono]	to make someone look a fool
sputtanarsi [spoot'tanarsee]	to make a fool of yourself

WARNING! SLANG

NUMBSKULLS & NITWITS

È un po' svitato. [eh oon po zveetato]	He/She has a screw loose.
È fuori di testa. [eh fworee dee testa]	He's/She's a sandwich short of a picnic.
sclerare [sklairareh]	to freak out
scemo/imbecille [shemo/eembecheel'leh]	idiot/moron
È un tordo. [eh oon tordo]	He's/She's a jerk. (lit: a thrush)
tonno [ton'no]	a klutz/a blunderer (lit: tuna)
È un esaltato. [eh oon ezaltato]	He's/She's crazy.
essere fissato [es'saireh fees'sato]	to be obsessed with something

MORE INSULTS

tamarro [tamar'ro]	an uncool, badly dressed guy
un/a fighetto/a [oon/a feeget'to/a]	a snob m/f
È un gasato. [eh oon gazato]	He's/She's a boaster/a blowhard.
cafone [kafoneh]	yokel/oaf/ redneck/jerk
rompicoglioni [rompeekol-yonee]	a pain in the arse/ass
dare i nervi/rompere i coglioni	to completely piss someone off
[dareh ee nairvee/rompaireh ee kol-yon-ee]	
leccare il culo a qc [lek'kareh eel koolo a kwalkoono]	to kiss someone's ass/arse
leccaculo [lek'ka-koolo]	arse kisser/ass licker
pirla [peerla]	idiot
coglione [kol-yoneh]	arse/ass hole
Che testa di cazzo! [keh testa dee kat'so]	What a dickhead!
stronzo [stront-so]	son of a bitch
pezzo di merda [pet'so dee mairda]	scumbag
un vecchio porco [oon vek'kyo porko]	a dirty old man
cornuto [kornooto]	a cuckold
terrone [tair'roneh]	a southern Italian (lit: earth muncher)
polentone [polentoneh]	a northern Italian (lit: polenta muncher)

*

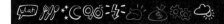

UNMENTIONABLES

il gabinetto/il cesso [eel gabeenet'to/eel ches'so] toilet/can/bog
Che tanfo! [keh tanfo] What a stink!
fare la pipì/pisciare [fareh la peepee/peeshareh] to pee/wee/piss
fare la cacca [fareh la kak'ka] to shit
avere la cacarella [avaireh la kakarel'la] to have diarrhoea/the shits
scoreggiare [skorej'jareh] to fart/let one go
ruttare [root'tareh] to burp/belch
vomitare l'anima [vomeetareh laneema] to vomit (lit: to vomit out your soul)

MONEY

◼CASH◼

i soldi/i quattrini/la grana/il denaro money/cash/moolah/dough
  [ee soldee/ee kwat'treenee/la grana/eel denaro]
gli spiccioli/spicci [l-yee speet'chyolee/speet'chee] change
un gruzzolo [oon groot'solo] a pile of money/a chunk of change

◼RICH OR BROKE◼

nuotare nell'oro [nwotareh nel'loro] to be swimming in money (lit: gold)
ricco sfondato [reek'ko sfondato] filthy rich
fare soldi a palate [fareh soldee a palateh] to make megabucks
È un figlio/una figlia di papà. He/she was born with a silver spoon
  [eh oon feel-yo/oona feel-ya dee papa]   in his/her mouth.
un sacco/un mucchio di soldi a heap of cash/a pile of money
  [oon sak'ko/oon mook'kyo dee soldee]

Fa il mantenuto/la mantenuta. He's/She's a kept man/woman.
  [fa eel mantenooto/la mantenoota]

È uno strozzino. [eh oono strot'seeno] He's/She's a shark/a racketeer.
spilorcio [speelorch-yo] stingy/mean
È un pidocchio. [eh oon peedok'kyo] He's/She's a miser. (lit: a louse)
uno scroccone [oono skrok'koneh] a freeloader/a leech
Ha le mani bucate. [a leh manee booikateh] Money slips through his/her fingers.
   (lit: he's/she's has holes in his/her hands)

essere al verde/in bolletta to be strapped for cash, to be broke
  [es'saireh al vairdeh/een bol'let'ta]   (essere al verde = lit: to be on the green)

WARNING! SLANG

◼ PRICEY OR PEANUTS

Costa una fortuna/un occhio della testa.
[kosta oona fortoona/oon ok'kyo del'la testa]

un prezzo sfacciato [oon pret'so sfat'chato]
svenarsi [zvenarsee]
un (vero) affare/un affarone
[oon (vairo) af'fareh/oon af'faroneh]
un prezzo stracciato [oon pret'so strat'chato]
Te lo tirano dietro. [teh lo teerano dyetro]

a sbafo [a zbafo]
Non vale un fico secco. [non valeh oon feeko sek'ko]

It costs a fortune.

an outrageous price
to pay an arm and a leg
a bargain/a steal

a bargain/a ridiculously low price
It costs next to nothing.
(lit: they're throwing it after you)*
free (of charge)
That's not worth shit. (lit: a dry fig)

◼ SPENDING & EARNING

nuovo di pacca [nwovo dee pak'ka]
un conto salato [oon konto salato]
tirare sul prezzo [teerareh sool pret'so]
scroccare [skrok'kareh]
farsi spennare [farsee spen'nareh]
I conti non tornano. [ee kontee non tornano]
fare i portoghesi [fareh ee porto-geh-see]
Offro io! [of'fro ee-yo]
fare alla romana [fareh al'la romana]

brand-spanking new
an steep bill/check
to haggle/bargain
to scrounge/cadge/bum
to get fleeced/ripped off
The figures don't add up.
to use a service without paying
This is on me!/It's my treat!
to go Dutch (lit: Roman)

WORK

fare una levataccia [fareh oona levatat'cha]
sgobbare [zgob'bareh]
rimboccarsi le maniche [reembok'karsee leh maneekeh]

to get up at the crack of dawn
to work hard/slog away
to roll up one's sleeves

*

Si è fatto in quattro. [see eh fat'to een kwat'tro] — He's/She's worked to the max.

Ci vuole olio di gomito. [chee vwoleh ol-yo dee gomeeto] — It needs a bit of elbow grease.

fare una fatica bestiale [fareh oona fateeka best-yaleh] — to work super hard

Si è fatto un culo/un mazzo così! — He's/She's worked his arse/ass off.

[see eh fat'to oon koolo/oon mat'so kosee]

stacanovista [stakanoveesta] — workaholic

ammazzarsi di lavoro [am'mat'sarsee dee lavoro] — to work oneself to death

È uno scioperato/un fancazzista. — He/She doesn't want to work.

[eh oono shopairato/oon fankat'seesta]

girarsi i pollici [jeerarsee ee pol'leechee] — to twiddle your thumbs

cazzeggiare [kat'sej'jareh] — to laze around

fannullone [fan'nool'loneh] — slacker/idler/lazybones

bigiare [beejareh] — to skive/skip work

È un assenteista. [eh oon as'sent-ay-sta] — He's/She's a skiver.

Ha fatto un (gran) casino. [a fat'to oon (gran) kaseeno] — He/She has screwed up.

fare un cazziatone [fareh oon kat-sya-toneh] — to tell someone off

crumiro [kroomeero] — strike-breaker/scab

lavoro nero [lavoro nairo] — moonlighting/illegal employment

THE WEATHER

Fa freschetto. [fa fresket'to] — It's pretty cold.

Fa un freddo cane. [fa oon fred'do kaneh] — It's freezing cold/as cold as hell.

(lit: it's doing a dog-cold)

Che tempo di merda! [keh tempo dee mairda] — What shit weather!

Piove che Dio la manda. [pyoveh keh dee-yo la manda] — It's pouring with rain./It's pissing it down.

bagnato fradicio [ban-yato fradeech-yo] — soaking wet

Fa un caldo bestiale. [fa oon kaldo best-yaleh] — It's boiling hot/as hot as hell.

prendere la tintarella [prendaireh la teentarel'la] — to top up your tan

rosso come un peperone [ros'so komeh oon pepaironeh] — sunburned (lit: as red as a pepper)*

Che afa! [keh afa] — It's so close/muggy!

CREDITS

Cover photograph: Corbis/Atantide Phototravel: Stefano Amantini
Photos: Denis Pernath (pp. 2, 3, 6/7, 10/11, 20/21, 54/55, 78/79, 104/105);
gettyimages/Michael Brauner (pp. 3, 36/37); Cortina Hotel, Munich (pp. 68/69)
Illustrations: Mascha Greune, Munich
'Point & Show' Pictures/Photos: Lazi&Lazi; Food Collection; Comstock;
stockbyte, Fisch-Informationszentrum e.V.; Fotolia/Christian Jung;
Fotolia/ExQuisine; photos.com
Picture editors: Factor Product, Munich (pp. 2, 3, 6/7, 10/11, 20/21, 36/37,
54/55, 68/69, 78/79, 104/105); red.sign, Stuttgart (pp. 41–45)
'Point & Show' Pictures/Illustrations: Factor Product, Munich; HGV Hanseatische
Gesellschaft für Verlagsservice, Munich (pp. 44/45, 56, 58/59, 63, 73, 75)

1st Edition 2014
Worldwide Distribution: Marco Polo Travel Publishing Ltd, Pinewood, Chineham
Business Park, Crockford Lane, Basingstoke, Hampshire RG24 8AL, United
Kingdom. E-mail: sales@marcopolouk.com
© MAIRDUMONT GmbH & Co. KG, Ostfildern
© based on the PONS Italian Travel Phrasebook
© PONS GmbH, Stuttgart

Chief editor: Marion Zorn, MAIRDUMONT
Concept and project management: Carolin Schmid, C.C.SCHMID Munich

Edited by: Raffaella Marini, Munich
Editing: PONS GmbH, Stuttgart; Kristin Schimpf, MAIRDUMONT, Ostfildern;
Barbara Pflüger, Stuttgart

"Warning! Slang" Chapter:
Editing: MAIRDUMONT, Ostfildern; Bintang Buchservice GmbH, Berlin
Author: Eleonora Zoratti, Trierweiler

Translated from German by J. Andrews, jonandrews.co.uk
Phonetics by J. Andrews, jonandrews.co.uk
Typesetting & Prepress: M. Feuerstein, Wigel

Coverdesign: Factor Product, Munich
Design content: Zum goldenen Hirschen, Hamburg; red.sign, Stuttgart

Printed in Germany

> READY FOR ANYTHING

At the Doctor's, at the police station or at the bank:
when things get tricky or need to be sorted out fast,
this handy chapter will help you out.

BANK/BUREAU DE CHANGE

 Numbers: Inside front cover

Where's the nearest bank, please?	Scusi, dove posso trovare una banca? [skoozee, doveh pos'so trovareh oona banka]
I'd like to change... pounds (dollars) into euros.	Vorrei cambiare ... sterlina (dollari) in euro. [vor'ray kambyareh ... stairleena (dol'laree) een ayooro]

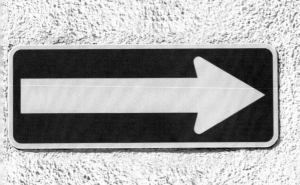

FROM
A TO Z

I'd like to change this traveller's cheque/check.	Vorrei riscuotere questo traveller's-cheque. [vor'ray reeskwo-taireh kwesto trav'lairz-shek]
May I see your...	Posso vedere … [pos'so vedaireh]
passport, please?	il Suo passaporto per favore? [eel soo-o pas'saporto pair favoreh]
identity card, please?	la Sua carta d'identità per favore? [la soo-a karta deedenteeta pair favoreh]
Sign here, please.	Firmi qui, per favore. [feermee kwee, pair favoreh]
The cashpoint won't accept my card.	Il bancomat non accetta la mia carta. [eel bankomat non at'chet'ta la mee-ya karta]
The cashpoint has swallowed my card.	Il bancomat non restituisce la mia carta. [eel bankomat non resteetoo-eesheh la mee-ya karta]

amount	importo [eemporto]
bank	banca [banka]
banknote	banconota [bankonota]
bureau de change	cambio [kambyo]
cash register	cassa [kas'sa]
cashpoint	cassa automatica prelievi [kas'sa owtomateeka prel-yevee], il bancomat [eel bankomat], sportello automatico [sportel'lo owtomateeko]
change n	gli spiccioli [l-yee speet'chyolee], moneta [moneta]
change (money) v	cambiare [kambyareh]
cheque/check	assegno [as'sen-yo]
coin	moneta [moneta]
counter	sportello [sportel'lo]
credit card	carta di credito [karta dee kredeeto]
currency	valuta [valoota]
exchange	cambio [kambyo]
exchange rate	corso dei cambi [korso day kambee]
form	modulo [modoolo]
money	denaro [denaro]
pay out v	pagare [pagareh]
pin number/code	numero segreto [noomairo segreto]
signature	firma [feerma]
traveller's cheque/check	assegno turistico [as'sen-yo tooreesteeko], il traveller's chèque [eel trav-lairz shek]

COLOURS

> Point & Show: page 4

beige	beige [beh-sh]
black	nero [nairo]
blue	blu [bloo]
brown	marrone [mar'roneh]
colourful	a colori [a koloree]
golden	color oro [kolor oro]
green	verde [vairdeh]
grey	grigio [greejo]
orange	arancione [aranch-yoneh]
pink	rosa [roza]
plain/monochrome	a tinta unita [a teenta ooneeta]

purple	lilla [leel'la]
red	rosso [ros'so]
silver	color argento [kolor arjento]
turquoise	turchese [toorkeseh]
violet	viola [vee-yola]
white	bianco [byanko]
yellow	giallo [jal'lo]

AT THE DOCTOR'S

▄▄▄INFORMATION | INFORMAZIONI [eenformat-syonee] ▄▄▄▄▄▄▄▄▄

Can you recommend	Mi può consigliare un buon …
a good…?	[mee pwo konseel-yareh oon bwon]
dentist	dentista? [denteesta]
dermatologist	dermatologo? [dairmatologo]
doctor	medico? [medeeko]
ear, nose and throat	otorinolaringoiatra?
specialist	[oto-reeno-lareen-goyatra]
eye specialist	oculista? [okooleesta]
general practitioner	medico generico? [medeeko jenaireeko]
gynaecologist	ginecologo? [jeenekologo]
neurologist	neurologo? [nay-oo-rologo]
pediatrician	pediatra? [pedee-yatra]
urologist	urologo? [oorologo]
Where's his/her	Dov'è il suo ambulatorio?
surgery/office?	[doveh eel soo-o amboolator-yo]

 Pharmacy: page 57, 58, 60

▄▄▄AT THE DOCTOR'S | DAL MEDICO [dal medeeko] ▄▄▄▄▄▄▄▄▄▄

What's the problem?	Che disturbi ha? [keh deestoorbee a]
It hurts here.	Ho dei dolori qui. [o day doloree kwee]
I've got a headache.	Ho mal di testa. [o mal dee testa]
I've got a sore throat.	Ho mal di gola. [o mal dee gola]
I've got a cough.	Ho la tosse. [o la tos'seh]
I'm allergic to…	Sono allergico a … [sono al'lairjeeko a]
antibiotics.	gli antibiotici. [l-yee anteebyoteechee]
bees.	le api. [leh apee]
pollen.	i pollini. [ee pol'leenee]

I'm vaccinated against...	Sono vaccinato contro ... [sono vat'cheenato kontro]
hepatitis A / B / A and B.	l'epatite A / B / A e B. [lepateeteh ah / bee / ah eh bee]
tetanus.	il tetano. [eel tetano]
typhoid.	il tifo. [eel teefo]
How often do I have to take it?	Quante volte devo prenderlo? [kwanteh volteh devo prendairlo]
I'm pregnant.	Sono incinta. [sono eencheenta]
I'm...	Sono ... [sono]
diabetic.	diabetico. [dee-yabeteeko]
epileptic.	epilettico. [epeelet'teeko]
Where does it hurt?	Dove fa male? [doveh fa maleh]
It's nothing serious.	Non è niente di grave. [non eh nyenteh dee graveh]
Can you give me/prescribe something for...?	Mi può dare/prescrivere qualcosa contro ...? [mee pwo dareh/preskreevaireh kwalkosa kontro]
I usually take...	Di solito prendo ... [dee soleeto prendo]

◼ AT THE DENTIST'S | DAL DENTISTA [dal denteesta] ◼◼◼◼◼◼◼◼◼◼

I've got (terrible) toothache.	Ho (un forte) mal di denti. [o (oon forteh) mal dee dentee]
This tooth (on the top row/	Questo dente (di sopra [kwesto denteh [dee sopra]/
on the bottom row/	di sotto [dee sot'to]/
in the front of my mouth/	davanti [davantee]/
in the back of my mouth)	in fondo [een fondo])
hurts.	fa male. [fa maleh]
I've lost a filling.	La piombatura è andata via. [la pyombatoora eh andata vee-ya]
I will have to fill the tooth.	Lo devo otturare. [lo devo ot'toorareh]
I will have to pull out the tooth.	Devo estrarlo. [devo estrarlo]
I've broken a tooth.	Mi si è rotto un dente. [mee see eh rot'to oon denteh]
I'd like an injection, please.	Mi faccia una puntura, per favore. [mee fat'cha oona poontoora, pair favoreh]

◼ IN HOSPITAL | IN OSPEDALE [een ospedaleh] ◼◼◼◼◼◼◼◼◼◼

| How long will I have to stay here? | Per quanto tempo devo stare qui? [pair kwanto tempo devo stareh kwee] |
| When can I get out of bed? | Quando potrò alzarmi? [kwando potro alt-sarmee] |

abdomen	l'addome m [lad'domeh]
abscess	accesso [at'ches'so]
AIDS	AIDS m [aee-dee-es'seh/aydz]
allergy	allergia [al'lairja]
anaesthetic	anestesia [anestezee-ya]
ankle	malleolo [mal'layolo]

appendix	l'appendice f [lap'pendeecheh]
arm	braccio [brat'chyo]
artificial limb	la protesi [la protezee]
asthma	l'asma m/f [lazma]
back	schiena [skyena]
backache	il dolore alla schiena [eel doloreh al'la skyena]
bandage	fasciatura [fash-yatoora]
belly	il ventre [eel ventreh]
blackout	svenimento [zveneemento]
bladder	vescica [vesheeka]
bleed v, blood	sanguinare [san-gweenareh], il sangue [eel san-gweh]
blood poisoning	setticemia [set'teechemee-ya]
blood pressure (high/low)	la pressione sanguigna (alta/bassa) [la pres'syoneh san-gween-ya [alta/bas'sa]]
bone	osso [os'so]
brain	cervello [chairvel'lo]
brain hemorrhage	apoplessia cerebrale [apoples'see-ya chaire-braleh]
breathe v	respirare [respeerareh]
broken	rotto [rot'to]
bronchitis	la bronchite [la bronkeeteh]
bruise, bruising	la contusione [la kontooz-yoneh]
burn n	l'ustione f [loost-yoneh]
bypass	bypass m [baee-pass]
catch a cold	prendere freddo [prendaireh fred'do], raffreddarsi [raf'fred'darsee]
chest	petto [pet'to]
chickenpox	varicella [vareechel'la]
chills/shivering	i brividi [ee breeveedee]
circulatory disorder	disturbi m circolatori [deestoorbee cheerkolatoree]
cold	il raffreddore [eel raf'fred'doreh]
colic	colica [koleeka]
collarbone	clavicola [klaveekola]
concussion	la commozione cerebrale [la kom'mot-syoneh chairebraleh]
constipation	la costipazione [la kosteepat-syoneh], stitichezza [stee-tee-ket'sa]
contagious	contagioso [kontajoso]
cough	la tosse [la tos'seh]
cramp	crampo [krampo]
cut n	ferita da taglio [faireeta da tal-yo]
diabetes	il diabete [eel dee-yabeteh]
diarrhoea	diarrea [dee-yar'raya]
difficulty breathing	difficoltà di respirazione [deef'feekolta dee respeerat-syoneh]
digestion	la digestione [la deejest-yoneh]
dizziness	le vertigini [leh vairteejeenee]

dress (a wound) v	fasciare [fash-yareh]
ear	orecchio [orek'kyo]
eardrum	membrana del timpano [membrana del teempano]
examination	l'esame m [lezameh]
extract v	togliere [tol-yaireh], estrarre [estrar'reh]
eye	occhio [ok'kyo]
face	faccia [fat'cha]
faint n	svenimento [zveneemento]
fever	la febbre [la feb'breh]
filling	piombatura [pyombatoora]
finger	dito [deeto]
flu	influenza [eenfloo-ent-sa]
food poisoning	l'intossicazione f da alimenti [leentos'seekat-syoneh da aleementee]
foot	il piede [eel pyedeh]
fracture	frattura ossea [frat'toora os'saya]
fungal infection	la micosi [la meekozee]
gall bladder	la cistifellea [la cheesteefel'laya]
German measles	rosolia [rozol-ya]
gullet	esofago [ezofago]
hand	la mano [la mano]
head	testa [testa]
headache	il mal di testa [eel mal dee testa]
heart	il cuore [eel kworeh]
heart attack	attacco cardiaco [at'tak'ko kardee-yako], infarto [eenfarto]
heart defect	difetto cardiaco [deefet'to kardee-yako]
heart trouble	i disturbi cardiaci [ee deestoorbee kardee-yachee]
hernia	l'ernia [lairnee-ya]
herpes	l'herpes m [lairpes]
hip	anca [anka]
HIV positive	sieropositivo [syairo-pozeeteevo]
hospital	l'ospedale m [lospedaleh]
hurt v	far male [far maleh]
ill/sick adj	malato [malato]
illness	malattia [malat'tee-ya]
indigestion	l'indigestione f [leendeejest-yoneh]
infection	l'infezione f [leenfet-syoneh]
inflammation	l'infiammazione f [leenf-yam'mat-syoneh]
inflammation of the (middle) ear	l'otite f [loteeteh]
injection	siringa [seereen-ga]
injure v, injury	ferire [faireereh], ferita [faireeta]
intestines	intestino [eentesteeno]
jaundice	itterizia [eet'taireet-sya]

joint	l'articolazione f [larteekolat-syoneh]
kidney stone	calcolo renale [kalkolo renaleh]
knee	ginocchio [jeenok'kyo]
leg	gamba [gamba]
lip	labbro [lab'bro]
liver	fegato [fegato]
lower back pain	la lombaggine [la lombaj'jeeneh]
lung	il polmone [eel polmoneh]
Lyme disease	borreliosi f [bor'rel-yozee]
measles	morbillo [morbeel'lo]
meningitis	la meningite [la meneenjeeteh]
menstruation	la mestruazione [la mestroo-at-syoneh]
migraine	emicrania [emeekranee-ya]
miscarriage	aborto [aborto]
mouth	bocca [bok'ka]
mumps	gli orecchioni [l-yee orek'kyonee]
muscle	muscolo [mooskolo]
neck	collo [kol'lo]
nephritis (kidney inflammation)	la nefrite [la nefreeteh]
nerve, nervous	nervo [nairvo], nervoso [nairvoso]
nose	naso [naso]
nurse	infermiera [eenfairm-yaira]
operation	l'operazione f [lopairat-syoneh]
pacemaker	il cardiostimolatore [eel kardee-yo-steemolatoreh], il pacemaker [eel payss-maykair]
pain	i dolori [ee doloree]
paralysis	la paralisi [la paraleezee]
poisoning	avvelenamento [av'velenamento]
polio	la polio(melite) [la pol-yo-(meleeteh)]
pregnant, pregnancy	incinta [eencheenta], la gravidanza [la graveedant-sa]
prescribe	prescrivere [preskreevaireh]
pull/strain (a muscle)	stiramento [steeramento]
pulse	polso [polso]
pus	il pus [eel poos]
rash	l'eruzione f cutanea [lairoot-syoneh kootan-aya], l'esantema m [lezantema]
reception	accettazione [at'chet'tat-syoneh]
rheumatism	i reumatismi [ee ray-oomateezmee]
rib	costola [kostola]
salmonella	la salmonellosi [la salmonel'lozee]
scar	la cicatrice [la cheeka-tree-cheh]
scarlet fever	scarlattina [skarlat'teena]
sciatica	sciatica [sh-yateeka]

sexual organs	gli organi genitali [l-yee organee jeneetalee]
shin	tibia [teebya]
shoulder	spalla [spal'la]
sick/ill adj	malato [malato]
sinusitis	la sinusite [la seenoozeeteh]
skin	la pelle [la pel'leh]
skull	cranio [kran-yo]
sleeplessness	insonnia [eenson'nee-ya]
smallpox	vaiolo [va-yolo]
sore throat	mal di gola [mal dee gola]
specialist	lo specialista [lo spechaleesta]
sprained	slogato [zlogato]
sting	punto [poonto], puntura [poontoora]
stomach, stomachache	stomaco [stomako], il mal di stomaco [eel mal dee stomako]
stools	le feci [leh fechee]
stroke	colpo apoplettico [kolpo apoplet'teeko]
sunstroke	colpo di sole [kolpo dee soleh]
surgery	orario di visita [orar-yo dee veezeeta]
sweat v	sudare [soodareh]
swelling	il gonfiore [eel gonf-yoreh], la tumefazione [la toomefat-syoneh]
swollen	gonfio [gonf-yo]
temperature (fever)	la febbre [la feb'breh]
tetanus	tetano [tetano]
throat	gola [gola]
tick	zecca [tsek'ka]
toe	dito del piede [deeto del pyedeh]
tongue	lingua [leen-gwa]
tonsils	le tonsille [leh tonseel'leh]
tooth	il dente [eel denteh]
tooth decay	la carie [la kar-eeyeh]
torn ligament	strappo dei legamenti [strap'po day legamentee]
typhoid	tifo [teefo]
ulcer	ulcera [oolchaira]
ultrasonic scan	l'esame m con ultrasuoni [lezameh kon ooltra-swonee], ecografia [ekografee-ya]
unconscious	privo di sensi [preevo dee sensee]
urine	urina [ooreena]
vaccination	la vaccinazione [la vat'cheenat-syoneh]
venereal disease	malattia venerea [malat'tee-ya venair-aya]
vomit v	vomitare [vomeetareh]
waiting room	sala d'aspetto [sala daspet'to]
wind n	flatulenza [flatoolent-sa]
wound	ferita [faireeta]
X-ray	radiografare [radee-yografareh]

INTERNET CAFÉS

Is there an Internet café near here?	C'è un internet café qui vicino?
	[cheh oon eentairnet kafeh kwee veecheeno]
What does it cost for an hour/a quarter of an hour?	Quanto costa un'ora/un quarto d'ora?
	[kwanto kosta oon-ora/oon kwarto dora]
Can I Skype here?	Posso skypare qui da Lei? [pos'so skaee-pareh kwee da lay]
Can I charge my device here?	Posso ricaricare da Lei il mio apparecchio?
	[pos'so reekaree-kareh da lay eel mee-yo ap'parek'kyo]
Do you have the right kind of charger for me?	Ha il caricatore giusto per me?
	[a eel kareekatoreh joosto pair meh]
Can I print out a page?	Posso stampare una pagina? [pos'so stampareh oona pajeena]
I can't get a connection here.	Non riesco a connettermi. [non ree-yesko a kon'net'tairmee]
Can I burn some photos from my digital camera onto CD here?	Mi potrebbe masterizzare su CD delle foto scaricate dalla mia fotocamera digitale? [mee potreb'beh mastaireet'sareh soo chee-dee del'leh foto skareekateh dal'la mee-ya fotokamaira deejeetaleh]
Do you have a headset for making phone calls?	Ha anche un headset per telefonare?
	[a ankeh oon ed-set pair telefonareh]

LOST & FOUND

Where's the lost property office, please?	Per favore, dov'è l'ufficio oggetti smarriti?
	[pair favoreh, doveh loof'feechyo oj'jet'tee zmar'reetee]
I've lost...	Ho perso ... [o pairso]
I left my handbag on the train.	Ho lasciato la (mia) borsa sul treno.
	[o lash-yato la (mee-ya) borsa sool treno]
Please let me know if it's handed in.	Per favore, se vengono riconsegnati/ritrovati, me lo faccia sapere. [pair favoreh, seh ven-gono reekonsen-yatee/ reetrovatee, meh lo fat'cha sapaireh]
Here's the address of my hotel/my home address.	Ecco l'indirizzo del mio albergo/l'indirizzo di casa.
	[ek'ko leendeereet'so del mee-yo albairgo/leendeereet'so dee kasa]

MAIL

Where's...	Per favore, dov'è ... [pair favoreh, doveh]
...the nearest post office, please?	... l'ufficio postale più vicino?
	[loof'feechyo postaleh pyoo veecheeno]
...the nearest postbox (mailbox), please?	... la prossima cassetta postale?
	[la pros'seema kas'set'ta postaleh]

How much does it cost to send a letter.../postcard...	Quanto costa una lettera .../una cartolina ... [kwanto kosta oona let'taira .../oona kartoleena ...]
to the UK?/to the US?/to Ireland?/to Canada?	per il Regno Unito?/per gli Stati Uniti?/per la Irlanda?/ per le Canada? [pair eel ren-yo ooneeto/pair l-yee statee ooneetee/ pair la eerlanda/pair leh kanada]
I'd like to send this letter by airmail/express.	Questa lettera con posta aerea/per espresso, per favore. [kwesta let'taira kon posta a-airaya/pair espres'so, pair favoreh]

address	indirizzo [eendeereet'so]
addressee	destinatario [desteenatar-yo]
by airmail	via aerea [vee-ya a-airaya]
central post office	posta centrale [posta chentraleh]
charge n	tariffa [tareef'fa]
collection	levata [levata]
counter	sportello [sportel'lo]
envelope	busta [boosta]
express letter	espresso [espres'so]
fill in	compilare [kompeelareh]
form	modulo [modoolo]
letter	lettera [let'taira]
parcel	pacco [pak'ko]
post code	CAP (codice di avviamento postale) [chee-ah-pee (kodeecheh dee av've-yamento postaleh)]
post office	ufficio postale [oof'feechyo postaleh]
post/mail v	spedire [spedeereh]
postage	affrancatura [af'frankatoora]
postbox/mailbox	cassetta postale [kas'set'ta postaleh]
postcard	cartolina postale [kartoleena postaleh]
sender	il mittente [eel meet'tenteh]
stamp	francobollo [frankobol'lo]
stamp v	affrancare [af'frankareh]
weight	peso [peso]

ON THE PHONE

I'd like...	Vorrei ... [vor'ray]
a phone card.	una scheda telefonica. [oona skeda telefoneeka]
to reverse the charges.	fare una telefonata a carico del destinatario. [fareh oona telefonata a kareeko del desteenatar-yo]
an international telephone card, please.	una carta telefonica internazionale, per favore. [oona karta telefoneeka eentairnat-syonaleh, pair favoreh]

What's the national/ area code for...?	Qual è il prefisso di ...? [kwal eh eel prefees'so dee]
I'd like to phone...	Vorrei telefonare in ... [vor'ray telefonareh een]
How much does it cost per minute?	Quanto costa al minuto? [kwanto kosta al meenooto]
This is... speaking.	Qui parla ... [kwee parla]; (the person receiving the call usually answers): Pronto? [pronto]
Hello, who's speaking?	Pronto, con chi parlo? [pronto, kon kee parlo]
Can I speak to Mr/Mrs..., please?	Scusi, potrei parlare con il signor/la signora ...? [skoozee, potray parlareh kon eel seen-yor/la seen-yora]
answer the phone	rispondere al telefono [reespondaireh al telefono]
call v	telefonare [telefonareh]
charge	tariffa [tareef'fa]
charger	il cavo carica [eel kavo kareeka]
connection n	la comunicazione [la komooneekat-syoneh]
dial v	formare il numero [formareh eel noomairo]
directory enquiries	le informazioni [leh eenformat-syonee]
engaged	occupato [ok'koopato]
international call	la comunicazione internazionale [la komooneekat-syoneh eentairnat-syonaleh]
line	telefonata [telefonata]
local call	telefonata urbana [telefonata oorbana]

LOCAL KNOWLEDGE

Insider Tips

"Pronto"

Italians have an efficient way of answering the phone. If you ring someone up, they'll often answer by simply saying: *"Pronto!?"* [pronto]. This excellent little word punches well above its weight - it essentially means "Hello, I'm ready to listen. What can I do for you?" Simple but effective!

Mobile/Cell Phones

Italian newspaper kiosks and tobacconists sell special phone cards for mobile/cell phones alongside the usual range of phone cards available for landlines (*Carta telefonica internazionale per telefono fisso* [karta telefoneeka eentairnat-syon-aleh pair telefono fees'so]).

long-distance call	interurbana [eentairoorbana]
make a phone call	telefonare [telefonareh]
mobile phone	telefono portatile [telefono portateeleh],
	il cellulare/telefonino [eel chel'loolareh/telefoneeno]
national/area code	prefisso [prefees'so]
payphone	telefono a gettone [telefono a jet'toneh]
(phone) call	telefonata [telefonata]
phone box	cabina telefonica [kabeena telefoneeka]
phone call/conversation	la conversazione [la konvairsat-syoneh]
phone card	carta telefonica [karta telefoneeka]
phone number	numero telefonico [noomairo telefoneeko]
prepaid card	la scheda prepagata [la skeda prepagata]
reverse-charge/collect call	la comunicazione telefonica a carico del ricevente
	[la komooneekat-syoneh telefoneeka a kareeko del reecheventeh]
SIM card	la carta SIM [la karta seem]
smartphone	lo smartphone [lo zmartfon]
telephone	telefono [telefono]
telephone directory	elenco telefonico [elenko telefoneeko]

▌MOBILE PHONE
▌IL CELLULARE/TELEFONINO [eel chel'loolareh/telefoneeno]

There's nothing left on my prepaid card.	La mia scheda prepagata è scarica. [la mee-ya skeda prepagata eh skareeka]
I'd like to top up my card.	Vorrei ricaricare la mia scheda. [vor'ray reekareekareh la mee-ya skeda]
A prepaid card (for [network provider]), please.	Vorrei una scheda prepagata (di [società di telefonia mobile]) [vor'ray oona skeda prepagata [dee [soch-yeta dee telefonee-ya mobeeleh]]]
How much call time do I get with a card for [amount of money]?	Quanti minuti posso parlare con una carta da …? [kwantee meenootee pos'so parlareh kon oona karta da]
What region is this SIM card valid for?	Per quale zona vale questa SIM? [pair kwaleh dzona valeh kwesta seem]
Please give me a price list/ the tarif information.	Potrebbe darmi una panoramica sulle tariffe? [potreb'beh darmee oona panorameeka sool'leh tareef'feh]
Have you got prepaid cards for [network provider]?	Ha delle carte prepagate della …? [a del'leh karteh prepagateh del'la]
My battery's empty. Do you have a charger I could use?	Il mio accumulatore è scarico. Ha un cavo per ricaricarlo? [eel mee-yo ak'koomoolatoreh eh skareeko. a oon kavo pair reekareekarlo]

TAKING PHOTOS

 Point & Show: page 59

Do you mind if I take a picture of you?	La posso fotografare? [la pos'so fotografareh]
Am I allowed to take pictures here?	È permesso fotografare qui? [eh pairmes'so fotografareh kwee]
Would you mind taking a photo of us?	Le dispiacerebbe farci una foto? [leh dees-pyach-aireb'beh farchee oona foto]
Just press this button.	Prema questo pulsante, per favore. [prema kwesto poolsanteh, pair favoreh]
That's very kind.	Molto gentile (of you = da parte Sua). [molto jenteeleh (da parteh soo-a)]

POLICE

Where's the nearest police station, please?	Dov'è la questura più vicina? [doveh la kwestoora pyoo veecheena]
I'd like to report...	Vorrei denunciare ... [vor'ray denoonchareh]
a theft./an accident.	un furto. [oon foorto]/un incidente. [oon eencheedenteh]
I've been mugged/raped.	Sono stato/a m/f, assalito/a m/f, violentato/a m/f. [sono stato/a, as'saleeto/a, vee-yolentato/a]
My... handbag/	Mi è stato/a rubato/a m/f ... [mee eh stato/a roobato/a]
wallet/	la borsa. [la borsa]/il portafoglio. [eel portafol-yo]/
camera/	la macchina fotografica. [la mak'keena fotografeeka]/
car has been stolen.	la macchina. [la mak'keena]
My car has been broken into.	La mia macchina è stata forzata. [la mee-ya mak'keena eh stata fort-sata]
I've lost...	Ho perso ... [o pairso]
My son/daughter is missing.	Mio figlio/Mia figlia è scomparso/a m/f. [mee-yo feel-yo/mee-ya feel-ya eh skomparso/a]
Can you help me, please?	Mi può aiutare, per favore? [mee pwo a-yootareh, pair favoreh]
I'd like to speak to a lawyer.	Vorei parlare con un avvocato. [voray parlareh kon oon av'vokato]
Please get in touch with the... British consulate/U.S. consulate/Irish consulate/ Canadian consulate.	Per favore, si rivolga al ... [pair favoreh, see reevolga al] ... consolato britannico/statunitense/irlandese/canadese [konsolato breetan'neeko/stat-oo-neetenseh/eerlandeseh/kanadeseh]

arrest v	arrestare [ar'restareh]
attack	l'aggressione f [lag'gres'syoneh]; assalto [as'salto]
bank card	carta assegni [karta as'sen-yee]
beat up v	picchiare [peek'kyareh]
break into/open	forzare [fort-sareh], scassinare [skas'seenareh]
car key	la chiave della macchina [la kyaveh del'la mak'keena]
car radio	l'autoradio f [lowtorad-yo]
cheque/check	assegno [as'sen-yo]
confiscate	sequestrare [sekwestrareh]
court	tribunale m [treeboonaleh]
crime	delitto [deleet'to]
documents	i documenti [ee dokoomentee]
drugs	gli stupefacenti [l-yee stoopefachentee]
harass	infastidire [eenfasteedeereh]
judge	giudice m/f [joodeecheh]
key	la chiave [la kyaveh]
lawyer	avvocato [av'vokato]
lose	perdere [pairdaireh]
money	denaro [denaro]
papers	i documenti [ee dokoomentee]
passport, identity card	passaporto [pas'saporto], carta d'identità [karta deedenteeta]
pickpocket	borsaiolo [borsa-yolo], lo scippatore [lo sheep'patoreh]
police	polizia [poleet-see-ya]
policeman/policewoman	l'agente m/f [lajenteh]; (traffice) il vigile/la vigilessa [eel veejeeleh/la veejeeles'sa]
prison	la prigione [la preejoneh]
purse	borsellino [borsel'leeno]
rape	violenza (carnale) [vee-yolent-sa (karnaleh)], stupro [stoopro]
report v	denunciare [denoonchareh]
theft	furto [foorto]
thief	ladro [ladro]
wallet	portafoglio [portafol-yo]

TOILETS & BATHROOMS

Where is the toilet, please?	Scusi, dov'è il bagno? [skoozee, doveh eel ban-yo]
May I use your toilet?	Scusi, ma dovrei andare in bagno. Posso? [skoozee, ma dovray andareh een ban-yo. pos'so]
Could you give me the key for the toilet, please?	Potrebbe darmi la chiave per il bagno, per favore? [potreb'beh darmee la kyaveh pair eel ban-yo, pair favoreh]
The toilet is blocked.	Il gabinetto è intasato. [eel gabeenet'to eh eentasato]

clean	pulito [pooleeto]
dirty	sporco [sporko]
Gents (toilet for men)	Signori m [seen-yoree]
Ladies (toilet for women)	Signore f [seen-yoreh]
soap	il sapone [eel saponeh]
toilet paper	carta igienica [karta eej-yeneeka]
towel	asciugamano [ashoogamano]
washbasin	lavabo [lavabo], lavandino [lavandeeno]

TRAVELLING WITH KIDS

Do you have children's portions?	Avete anche porzioni per bambini? [aveteh ankeh port-syonee pair bambeenee]
Could you warm up the bottle, please?	Mi potrebbe riscaldare il biberon, per favore? [mee potreb'beh reeskaldareh eel beebairon, pair favoreh]
Is there a baby changing room?	C'è un fasciatoio? [cheh oon fash-yatoyo]
Where can I breastfeed my baby?	Dove posso allattare? [doveh pos'so al'lat'tareh]
Please bring another high chair.	Mi porti ancora un seggiolone, per favore. [mee portee ankora oon sej'joloneh, pair favoreh]

armbands/water wings	il bracciale [eel brat'chaleh]
baby food	l'alimentazione f infantile [laleementat-syoneh eenfanteeleh]
baby monitor	il babyphone [eel baybee-fon]
baby changing table	fasciatoio [fash-yatoyo]
babysitter	baby-sitter m/f [babee-seet'tair]
bottle warmer	scaldabiberon m [skaldabeebairon]
child discount	riduzione f per bambini [reedoot-syoneh pair bambeenee]
child's safety seat	seggiolino per l'auto [sej'joleeno pair lowto]
cot	lettino [let'teeno]
day care	assistenza ai bambini [as'seestent-sa aee bambeenee]
dummy	ciuccio [chyoot'chyo], succhietto [sook'kyet'to]
feeding bottle	il biberon [eel beebairon]
nappies/diapers	i pannolini [ee pan'noleenee]
paddling pool	sguazzatoio [zgwat'satoyo]
playground	campo giochi [kampo jokee]
toys	i giocattoli [ee jokat'tolee]
rubber ring	il salvagente [eel salvajenteh]

Weather: page 19
Numbers: Inside front cover
Time: page 16, 17

THE MOST IMPORTANT WORDS

The numbers printed after some words are there to point you to the relevant page in a related chapter.

Abbreviations used: adj = adjective; adv = adverb; n = noun; prep = preposition; v = verb; Am: = American English; Br: = British English; sing = singular; pl = plural

A

a un [oon], uno [oono], una [oona]

abandon v lasciare [lash-yareh], abbandonare [ab'bandonareh]

able: to be able to potere [potaireh], sapere [sapaireh]

about (approximately) circa [cheerka], quasi [kwazee]; (time: e.g. about 7 pm) circa [cheerka], attorno a [at'torno a]

absolutely assolutamente [as'solootamenteh]

accessible (for people with disabilities) idoneo per/a misura degli handicappati [eedonayo pair/a meezoora del-jee andeekap'patee]

accident incidente m [eencheedenteh] ➤ 25, disgrazia [deesgrat-sya]; (to have an accident) avere un incidente/infortunio [avaireh oon eencheedenteh/eenfortoon-yo]

accommodation alloggio [al'loj'jo]

accompany accompagnare [ak'kompan-yareh]

activity attività [at'teeveeta]; **activity holiday/vacation** vacanza attiva [vakant-sa at'teeva] ➤ 85

additional supplementare [soop'plementareh], addizionale [ad'deet-syonaleh]

address indirizzo [eendeereet'so] ➤ 116; (addressee) destinatario [desteen-atar-yo] ➤ 116

adjust rettificare [ret'teefeekareh], aggiustare [aj'joostareh]

Adriatic Sea Adriatico [adree-yateeko]

adult n adulto/adulta [adoolto/adoolta]

advance (in advance) in anticipo [een anteecheepo], con anticipo [kon anteecheepo]; (advance booking) prevendita [prevendeeta] ➤ 84

advise v consigliare [konseel-yareh]

aeroplane (airplane) aereo [a-air-ayo] ➤ 29

afraid: to be afraid of aver paura di [avair pow-ra dee]

after dopo [dopo]

afternoon pomeriggio [pomaireej'jo]; (in the afternoon) il pomeriggio [eel pomaireej'jo]

again di nuovo [dee nwovo]

against contro [kontro]

age n età [eta] ➤ 14

agency (office, bureau) agenzia [ajent-see-ya]

agree (believe the same) essere d'accordo [es'saireh dak'kordo], concordare [konkordareh]; (come to terms) conciliare [koncheel-yareh]; (consent to) acconsentire [ak'konsenteereh]

air aria [ar-ya]

airport aeroporto [a-airoporto]

alcohol level (blood) per mille [pair meel'leh]

all tutto [toot'to], tutta [toot'to], tutti pl [toot'tee], tutte pl [toot'teh]

allow permettere [pairmet'taireh]

alone solo [solo]

along prep lungo [loon-go]

already già [ja]

also anche [ankeh], pure [pooreh]

altitude altezza [altet'sa]

always sempre [sempreh]

ambulance autoambulanza [owto-amboolant-sa]

American (man/woman) americano/americana [amaireekano/amaireekana]

among tra [tra], fra [fra], in mezzo a [een met'so a]; (among others) fra gli altri [fra l-yee altree]

amount (money) importo [eemporto], somma [som'ma] ➤ 111

and e [eh]

angry arrabbiato [ar'rab'byato], in collera [een kol'laira]

animal animale m [aneemaleh]

annoy infastidire [eenfastee-deereh] ➤ 115; (annoying) seccante [sek'kanteh]; (to be annoyed about/at) arrabbiarsi per [ar'rab'byarsee pair]

another altro [altro], un altro [oon altro]

apart from inoltre [eenoltreh]

apartment appartamento [ap'partamento]

apologize scusarsi [skoozar-see] ➤ 12

appetite appetito [ap'peteeto]

appointment (meeting) appuntamento [ap'poontamento], riunione f [ree-oon-yoneh] ➤ 15; (deadline) scadenza [skadent-sa]

area area [ar-aya], zona [dzona]

area code prefisso [prefees'so] ➤ 117

around prep attorno [at'torno], intorno [eentorno]

arrival arrivo [ar'reevo] ➤ 30, 32

arrive v arrivare [ar'reevareh] ➤ 32

as far as I'm concerned da parte mia [da parteh mee-ya]

as if come se [komeh seh]

ask (s.o. for sth) chiedere (qc a qlc) [kyed-aireh [kwalkosa a kwalkoono]]

at (time) alle [al'leh]

at home a casa [a kasa]

at least per lo meno [pair lo meno]

attack v attaccare [at'tak'kareh]

DICTIONARY

aunt   zia [tsee-ya]
authorities (police, etc.)   autorità pubblica [owtoreeta poob'bleeka]
available (on sale)   in vendita [een vendeeta]
average   adj medio [med-yo]; n mezzo [met'so]; (on average) in media [een med-ya]
awake adj   sveglio [zvel-yo]
away (gone)   via [vee-ya]

B

baby   neonato [nayonato] > 119
bachelor   scapolo [skapolo]
back (i.e. to be back)   all'indietro [al'leen-dyetro]
bad adj   cattivo [kat'teevo]; **badly** adv   male [maleh]; (bad weather) brutto [broot'to]
baggage (luggage)   bagaglio [bagal-yo] > 29, 32
ball   (sports) palla [pal'la]; (dance) ballo [bal'lo]
band (music)   banda (musicale) [banda (moozeekaleh)]
bank   banca [banka] > 104
bar   il bar [eel bar], osteria [ostairee-ya] > 39, 82
bathing/seaside resort   località turistica di mare [lokaleeta tooreesteeka dee mareh]
bay (sea, etc.)   golfo [golfo]
be v   essere [es'saireh]
beach   spiaggia [spee-yaj'ja] > 84
beautiful   bello [bel'lo]
because   perché [pairkeh]; (because of) a causa di [a kowsa dee], per [pair]
become v   divenire [deeven-eereh]
bed   letto [let'to]
bedroom   camera [kamaira] > 6, 74
bee   ape f [apeh]
before   prima [preema], prima di [preema dee]
begin   iniziare [eeneet-syareh]; (beginning) inizio [eeneet-syo]
behind   dietro [dyetro]
believe   credere [kredaireh]
bell   campanello [kampanel'lo]
belong v   appartenere [ap'partenaireh]
below   sotto [sot'to]
bench   panchina [pankeena]
bend (in a road, etc.)   curva [koorva]
beside/by prep   vicino a [veecheeno a]
between   tra [tra], fra [fra]
bicycle   bicicletta [beecheeklet'ta] > 23, 87
big   grande [grandeh]
bill n (Am: the check)   conto [konto]
birth   nascita [nasheeta]; (birthday) i compleanno [ee komplay-an'no] > 12; (birth place) luogo di nascita [lwogo dee nasheeta]
bit: a bit   un po' [oon po]
bite v   mordere [mordaireh]
black   nero [nairo]
blanket   coperta [kopairta], coltre f [koltreh], manto [manto]
blood   il sangue [eel san-gweh] > 109

blue   blu [bloo]
boat   barca [barka] > 88
body   corpo [korpo] > 108
boil v   bollire [bol'leereh]
book n   libro [leebro]
booking   la prenotazione [la prenotat-syoneh] > 6, 30, 83
border   frontiera [front-yaira], confine m [konfeeneh] > 22
boring   noioso [noyoso]
born   nato [nato]
boss n   capo [kapo]
both   entrambi [entrambee]
bottle n   bottiglia [bot'teel-ya]
bouquet   mazzo [mat'so]
boy   ragazzo [ragat'so]
boyfriend   ragazzo [ragat'so]
brakes n   freni m, pl [frenee] > 24
brand n (i.e. brand name)   marca [marka]
bread   il pane [eel paneh] > 43, 46, 64
break v   rompere [rompaireh]; (break open) forzare [fort-sareh], scassinare [skas'seenareh] > 118
breakdown (car, etc.)   guasto [gwasto] > 24, 25
breakfast   la prima colazione [la preema kolat-syoneh] > 46, 70
brief adj   breve [breveh]
bring   portare [portareh]; (bring along) portare con sè [portareh kon seh]
broad   largo [largo]
broken   rotto [rot'to]
brother   fratello [fratel'lo]
brother-in-law   cognato [kon-yato]
building   edificio [edeefeechyo] > 80
bureau de change   cambio [kamb-yo] > 104
burn v   bruciare [broochareh]
bus   l'autobus m [lowtoboos] > 34
business days   nei giorni m, pl feriali [nay jornee fair-ya-lee]
but   ma [ma]
buy v   comprare [komprareh]
by (i.e. written by)   di [dee]
bye!   ciao! [chow]

C

cabin   cabina [kabeena] > 33
café   caffè m [kaf'feh]
calculate v   calcolare [kalkolareh]; (add up/together) sommare [som'mareh]
calendar of events   calendario delle manifestazioni [kalendar-yo del'leh maneefestat-syoneh] > 83
call v   chiamare [kya-mareh]; (on the phone) telefonare [telefonareh]; (to be called) chiamarsi [kyamarsee]
calm n   pace f [pacheh]; (calm down) tranquillizzarsi [trankweel'leet'sarsee]

camping camping m [kam-peeng], campeggio [kampej'jo] ➤ 76; (campsite) (area di) campeggio [(ar-aya dee) kampej'jo]

Canada Canada [kanada]

Canadian (man/woman) canadese [kana-deseh]

cancel annullare [an'nool'lareh], disdire [deezdeereh] ➤ 29

capable: to be capable of essere capace di [es'saireh kapacheh dee]

car auto f [owto], macchina [mak'keena] ➤ 23

care: take care of occuparsi di [ok'kooparsee dee]

carry portare [portareh]

cash contanti m, pl [kontantee], denaro contante [denaro kontanteh], denaro liquido [denaro leekweedo]

cash register cassa [kas'sa]

cashpoint (ATM) il bancomat [eel bankomat], sportello [sportel'lo] ➤ 105

castle castello [kastel'lo] ➤ 80

cat gatto [gat'to]

caution (care) precauzione f [prekowt-syoneh]

ceiling soffitto [sof'feet'to]

celebration celebrazione f [chelebrat-syoneh]

cell phone (Br: mobile phone) il cellulare/telefonino [eel chel'loolareh/telefoneeno] ➤ 116

centre (Am: center) centro [chentro]

certain adj certo [chairto]; **certainly** adv certamente [chairtamenteh]

certify certificare [chairteefeekareh]

chair sedia [sed-ya]

change n (coins) gli spiccioli [l-yee speet'ch-yolee], moneta [moneta] ➤ 106

change v cambiare [kamb-yareh], modificare [modeefeekareh]; (a ticket) cambiare il biglietto [kamb-yareh eel beel-yet'to] ➤ 30; (money, trains) cambiare [kamb-yareh] ➤106

Channel (the English Channel) Canale m della Manica [kanaleh del'la maneeka]

channel (TV) canale m [kanaleh]

chapel cappella [kap'pel'la] ➤ 80

cheap non caro [non karo], economico [ekonomeeko], a buon mercato [a bwon mairkato]

cheat v ingannare [een-gan'nareh]

check v controllare [kontrol'lareh]; n (Br: bill) conto [konto];

cheerful allegro [al'legro]

cheese formaggi m, pl [formaj'jee] ➤ 43, 50, 64

chemist's/drug store profumeria [profoomairee-ya] ➤ 57, 58

cheque (Am: check) assegno [as'sen-yo] ➤ 106

child bambino [bambeeno]

choose scegliere [shel-yaireh]

Christian name il nome [eel nomeh] ➤ 22

church chiesa [kyeza] ➤ 80

cigarette sigaretta [seegaret'ta]

cinema il cinema [eel cheenema] ➤ 83

city centre centro [chentro]

city hall (Br: town hall) municipio [moonee-cheep-yo] ➤ 81

clean adj pulito [pooleeto]; v pulire [pooleereh]

clergyman/woman m il sacerdote [eel sachair-doteh], il prete [eel preteh]; f donna sacerdote [don'na sachair-doteh]

clever (intelligent) intelligente [eentel'leejenteh]

climate clima m [kleema]

climb v salire [saleereh]

clock orologio a parete [orolojo a pareteh]

closed chiuso [kyooso]

clothes abbigliamento [ab'beel-yamento] ➤ 62

coal carbone m [karboneh]

coast costa [kosta]

coffee caffè m [kaf'feh] ➤ 46, 52, 64

coin moneta [moneta]

cold adj freddo [fred'do]; (to be cold) aver freddo [avair fred'do]

collect v raccogliere [rak'kol-yaireh]

colour n (Am: color) tinta [teenta], il colore [eel koloreh]

come v venire [veneereh]; (come from) derivare [daireevareh], provenire [proveneereh], discendere [deeshendaireh]; (come in!) avanti! [avantee]

common adj comune [komooneh]

communication problems problemi m, pl di comunicazione [probleeme dee komooneekaat-syoneh]

company (business) ditta [deet'ta]

compare v comparare [komparareh], confrontare [konfrontareh]

compensation indennizzo [eenden'neet'so], risarcimento [ree-sarch-eemento]

complain reclamare [reklamareh], protestare [protestareh] ➤ 38, 70; (complain/moan about) lamentarsi di [lamentarsee dee]

complaint reclamo [reklamo] ➤ 38, 70

complete adj completo [kompleto]; **complete** adv interamente [eentairamenteh], completamente [kompletamenteh]

compliments complimenti m, pl [kompleementee] ➤ 13

computer shop/store negozio specializzato in computer [negot-syo spechaleet'sato een kompootair] ➤ 56, 59

concert concerto [konchairto] ➤ 83

concierge (porter) il portiere [eel port-yaireh]

condom preservativo [presairvateevo], profilattico [profeelat'teeko]

confirm confermare [konfairmareh]

confiscate sequestrare [sekwest-rareh]

confuse scambiare [skam-byareh]

congratulate congratularsi [kon-gratoolarsee], fare gli auguri [fareh l-yee owgooree]; (congratulations) auguri o [owgoor-yo] ➤ 12

connect (technology, etc.) connettere [kon'net'taireh]

connection (personal) relazione f [relat-syoneh],

rapporto [rap'porto], contatto [kontat'to]; (travel) coincidenza [ko-eencheedent-sa] **> 30, 32**

constitution (political) costituzione f [kostee-toot-syoneh]

consulate consolato [konsolato]

contact n contatto [kontat'to]; v contattare [kontat'tareh], mettersi in contatto [met'tairsee een kontat'to]

contents contenuto [kontenooto]

continue continuare [konteenoo-areh]

contraceptive n anticoncezionale m [anteekon-chet-syonaleh]

contract contratto [kontrat'to]

conversation conversazione f [konvairsat-syoneh]

cook v cucinare [koocheenareh]

cool (temp.) fresco [fresko]

corner angolo [an-golo]

corridor corridoio [kor'reedoyo]

corrupt corrotto [kor'rot'to]

cost costare [kostareh]

counter n (post office, etc.) sportello [sportel'lo] **> 106, 114**

country (nation) paese m [pa-yezeh]; (home/native country) patria [patree-ya]

country estate; country house tenuta in campagna [tenoota een kampan-ya]; casa di campagna [kasa dee kampan-ya]

couple (married) coppia [kop'pya]

course (lessons) corso [korso]; (meal) portata [portata], piatto [pyat'to]

court (law) tribunale [treeboonaleh] **> 118**

cousin cugino [koojeeno], cugina [koojeena]

credit card carta di credito [karta dee kredeeto] **> 54, 106**

criticize v criticare [kreeteekareh]

cross v (a road, etc.) attraversare [at'travairsareh]

cry (weep) piangere [pyan-jaireh]

culture cultura [kooltoora] **> 78**

curious curioso [koor-yoso]

currency valuta [valoota] **> 112**

current (electrical) corrente f (elettrica) [kor'renteh (elet'treeka)]

cushion cuscino [koosheeno]

customs (border control) dogana [dogana] **> 22**; (customs duty) i diritti doganali [ee deereet'tee doganalee]; (customs office) ufficio doganale [oof'feechyo doganaleh]; (customs officer) doganiere m/f [eel dogan-yaireh]

cut v tagliare [tal-yareh]

cutlery le posate [leh posateh]

cycle v andare in bicicletta [andareh een beecheeklet'ta] **> 23, 87**

■ **D** ▬▬▬▬▬▬▬▬▬▬▬▬▬▬▬▬▬

damage n danno [dan'no]; v danneggiare [dan'nej'jareh]; (harm) nuocere [nwochaireh]

damaged (faulty, defective) difettoso [deefet'toso] **> 24**

dance v ballare [bal'lareh] **> 82**; (dance hall) sala de ballo [sala deh bal'lo]

dangerous pericoloso [paireekoloso]

dark scuro [skooro]

date (appointment) appuntamento [ap'poontamento]; (calendar) data [data] **> 17**; (date of birth) data di nascita [data dee nasheeta] **> 22**

daughter figlia [feel-ya]

day giorno [jorno]; (day of arrival) giorno d'arrivo [jorno dar'reevo]

dead morto [morto]

dear adj (friend, etc.) caro [karo]

death morte f [morteh]

debt debito [debeeto]

decide decidere [decheedaireh]

decision risoluzione f [reesoloot-syoneh], decisione f [decheez-yoneh]

declare dichiarare [deek-ya-rareh]

deep profondo [profondo]; (low) basso [bas'so]

definite adj definitivo [defeeneeteevo]; **definitely** adv definitivamente [defeen-eeteeva-menteh]

degree (temperature, etc.) grado [grado]

demand v chiedere [kyed-aireh]

denomination (relig.) la confessione [la konfes'syoneh], la religione [la releejoneh]

dentist dentista [denteesta] **> 108**

departure partenza [partent-sa] **> 29, 34**

deposit (security deposit) cauzione f [kowt-syoneh]

deserve meritare [maireetareh]

destination meta [meta]

destroy distruggere [deestrooj'jaireh]

details (personal details) generalità pl [jenairaleeta]

develop v sviluppare [zveeloop'pareh]

dial v (phone number) formare il numero [formareh eel noomairo]

die v morire [moreereh]

difference differenza [deef'fairent-sa]

different adj differente [deef'fairenteh]; **differently** adv diverso [deevairso], diversamente [deevairsamenteh]

difficult difficile [deef'feecheeleh]

direction direzione f [deeret-syoneh]

director (manager) direttore m [deeret'toreh]

directory n elenco [elenko]

dirt n sporcizia [sporcheet-sya]; **dirty** adj sporco [sporko]

disabled toilets il bagno/la toilette per handicappati [eel ban-yo/la toylet'teh pair andeekap'patee]

disappointed deluso [deloozo]

disco discoteca [deeskoteka] **> 82**

discount sconto [skonto]

discover scoprire [skopreereh]

distance tratto [trat'to]

distant (far away) lontano [lontano]

distrust v diffidare (di qc/qlc) [deef'feedareh], non fidarsi (di qc/qlc) [non feedarsee]

disturb disturbare [deestoorbareh]; (disturbance) disturbo [deestoorbo]

diversion la deviazione [la devee-yat-syoneh]

dizzy vertiginoso [vairteejeenoso]; (dizziness) le vertigini [leh vairteejeenee]

do v fare [fareh]

doctor medico [medeeko], dottore m [dot'toreh] ➤ 107

dog cane m [kaneh]

door porta [porta]; (front door) portone m [portoneh]

double adj doppio [dop'pyo], adv doppiamente [dop'pyamenteh]

doubt sth dubitare di qc [doobeetareh dee kwalkosa]

downwards in giù [een joo]

dream v sognare [son-yareh]

dress v (a wound) fasciare [fash-yareh]; (dressing) fasciatura [fash-yatoora]

drink n bevanda [bevanda] ➤ 38, 45, 52, 64; v bere [baireh]

drive v guidare [gweedareh]

driving licence la patente [la patenteh]; (driving documents) i documenti [ee dokoomentee]

drunk ubriaco [oobree-yako]; (tipsy) un po' allegro [oon po al'legro]

drunk: get drunk ubriacarsi [oobree-yakarsee]

duration durata [doorata]

during durante [dooranteh]

duty dovere m [dovaireh]

E

early presto [presto]

earn v guadagnare [gwadan-yareh]

earth terra [tair'ra]

east est m [est]

easy facile [facheeleh]

eat mangiare [manjareh] ➤ 36, 64

edge n orlo [orlo]

edible commestibile [kom'mestee-beeleh]

education educazione f [edookat-syoneh]

effort (trouble) sforzo [sfort-so]

egg uovo [wovo]

either...or o ... o ... [o ... o ...]

electrical shop l'elettricista m [lelet'treecheesta] ➤ 56, 59

elevator ascensore m [ashensoreh]

email address indirizzo e-mail [eendeereet'so ee-ma-eel] ➤ 8

embassy ambasciata [ambash-yata]

emergency brake/exit/telephone freno/uscita/ telefono d'emergenza [freno/oosheeta/telefono demairjent-sa] ➤ 32, 30, 27

emphasis accento [at'chento]

employment impiego [eem-pyego]

empty vuoto [vwoto]

end v finire [feeneereh]

engaged: to get engaged to fidanzarsi con [feedant-sarsee kon]

engine (motor) il motore [eel motoreh] ➤ 24, 27

England Inghilterra [een-geeltair'ra]

English(man/woman) inglese [een-gleseh]

enjoy v godere [godaireh]

enough sufficiente [soof'feech-yenteh]

enquire informarsi [eenformarsee]

enter entrare [entrareh]; (a country) entrare in un paese [entrareh een oon pa-yezeh]

entertaining divertente [deevairtenteh]

entertainment divertimento [deevairteemento] ➤ 82

entrance n ingresso [een-gres'so]

environment ambiente m [am-byenteh]

et cetera e così via [eh kosee vee-ya], eccetera [et'chetaira]

Euro euro [ayoo-ro] ➤ 104

Europe Europa [ayoo-ropa]

European (man/woman) europeo/europea [ayoo-ropayo/ayoo-ropaya]

even adv pure [pooreh], magari [magaree]

evening sera [saira]

event avvenimento [av'veneemento]; (show, performance) manifestazione f [maneefestat-syoneh], spettacolo [spet'takolo]

every ogni [on-yee]; (every time) ogni volta [on-yee volta]

everyone ognuno [on-yoono]

everything tutto [toot'to]

everywhere dappertutto [dap'pairtoot'to]

evil cattivo [kat'teevo]

exact adj preciso [precheezo]; **exactly** adv esattamente [ezat'tamenteh], precisamente [precheezamenteh]

examination (inspection) l'esame m [lezameh]; (medical) visita medica [veezeeta medeeka]

examine controllare [kontrol'lareh]

example esempio [ezemp-yo]

except (apart from) eccetto [et'chet'to], tranne [tran'neh]

exchange cambiare [kamb-yareh]

exchange rate cambio [kamb-yo] ➤ 104

excuse n scusa [skooza]

exhausted esaurito [ezowreeto]

exit n uscita [oosheeta]; (motorway/highway) uscita [oosheeta], svincolo [zveenkolo]

expenses spese f, pl [speseh]

expensive caro [karo]

experienced adj esperto [espairto]

expire (voucher, etc.) svolgere [zvol-jaireh], svolgersi [zvol-jairsee]

explain spiegare [spee-yeg-areh]

extend v allungare [al'loon-gareh]; (time) prolungare [proloon-gareh]

extinguish spegnere [spen-yaireh]

F

factory fabbrica [fab'breeka]
faith fede f [fedeh]
faithful fedele [fedeleh]
fall v cadere [kadaireh]
family famiglia [fameel-ya]
far (distance) lungo [loon-go];
(far away) lontano [lontano]
farewell: say farewell prendere congedo
[prendaireh konjedo] ➤ 12
fashion moda [moda] ➤ 62
fast-food restaurant spuntino [spoon-teeno]
fat adj grosso [gros'so], spesso [spes'so];
(person) grasso [gras'so]; (swollen) gonfio [gonf-yo]; n grosso [gros'so]
father padre m [padreh]
fear n paura [powra]; v temere [temaireh]
fee tassa [tas'sa];
(professional charge) onorario [onorar-yo]
feel v sentire [senteereh]
feeling sentimento [senteemento]
feminine femminile [fem'meeneeleh]
festival (film, music) festival m [festeeval];
(street festival) celebrazione f [chelebrat-syoneh], festa [festa]
few poco [poko]
few: a few alcuni [alkoonee]
fiancé/fiancée fidanzato/fidanzata
[feedant-sato/feedant-sata]
field campo [kampo]
fill in/out (a form, etc.) compilare [kompeelareh]
film (movie) film m [feelm] ➤ 83;
(for a camera) pellicola [pel'leekola]
finally finalmente [feenalmenteh]
find v trovare [trovareh]
fine (financial penalty) ammenda [am'menda], multa [moolta]
finish v finire [feeneereh]; (finished) finito [feeneeto]
fire alarm segnalatore m d'incendio
[sen-yalatoreh deenchend-yo]
fire extinguisher estintore m [esteentoreh]
fire n fuoco [fwoko];
(building, forest, etc.) incendio [eenchend-yo]
fire service vigili m, pl del fuoco [veejeelee del fwoko], pompieri m, pl [pomp-yairee]
firewood legna da ardere [len-ya da ardaireh]
first aid pronto soccorso [pronto sok'korso]
first floor (Br: ground floor) pianoterra
[pyano-tair'ra], pianterreno [pyan-tair'reno]
first name il nome [eel nomeh] ➤ 22
firstly (first of all) prima [preema]
fish n pesce m [pesh-eh] ➤ 45, 49, 64
fishmonger pescivendolo [pesheevendolo]
flash (photo) flash m [flash]
flat adj piano [pyano]
flaw (personality, etc.) difetto [deefet'to]

flight volo [volo] ➤ 29, 30
flirt v flirtare [fleertareh] ➤ 15
floor (storey) piano [pyano];
(under foot) pavimento [paveemento]
flow v scorrere [skor'raireh]
flower fiore m [fyoreh]
fly v volare [volareh]; n (animal) mosca [moska]
follow seguire [seg-weer-eh];
(obey) ubbidire [oob'beedeereh]
food alimentari m, pl [aleementaree] ➤ 36, 64
for per [pair]
forbid v proibire [pro-eebaireh];
forbidden adj vietato [vye-tato]
foreign straniero [stran-yairo]; (foreigner) straniero
[stran-yairo], straniera [stran-yaira], forestiero m
[forest-yairo], forestiera f [forest-yaira]
forest bosco [bosko] ➤ 81
forget dimenticare [deementeekareh]
forgive perdonare [pairdonareh]
fork forchetta [forket'ta]
form (to fill in) formulario [formoolar-yo], modulo [modoolo]
fragile fragile [frajeeleh]
free (of charge) gratuito [gratweeto], gratis [gratees]
freeze congelare [konjelareh], gelare [jelareh]
frequently frequentemente [frekwentementeh], spesso [spes'so]
fresh fresco [fresko]
friend amico/amica [ameeko/ameeka]
friend: to be friends essere in amicizia
[es'saireh een ameecheet-sya]
friendly amichevole [ameekevoleh]
frighten spaventare [spaventareh];
(to be frightened) spaventato [spaventato]
from (origin) da [da], di [dee]; (time) da [da]
front: in front of davanti a [davantee a]
fruit la frutta [la froot'ta] ➤ 42, 46, 51, 64
full pieno [pyeno], completo [kompleto]
full (after food) sazio [sat-syo], satollo [satol'lo]
full board (accommodation) pensione completa
[pen-syoneh kompleta] ➤ 70, 72
fun divertimento [deevairteemento]
furious arrabbiato [ar'rab'byato], infuriato [eenfoor-yato]
furniture mobile m [mobeeleh]
fuse (electric) sicurezza [seekooret'sa]

G

garage (for repairs) officina [of'feecheena] ➤ 24;
(car storage) garage m [garajeh]
garbage n (Br: rubbish) immondizia [eem'mondeet-sya]
garden giardino [jardeeno]
gas (Br: petrol) benzina [bend-zeena] ➤ 23
gas station (Br: petrol station) stazione f, pl di
servizio [stat-syoneh dee sairveet-syo] ➤ 23, 28
gear (on a car, etc.) marcia [marcha]

gentleman signore m [seen-yoreh]
genuine vero [vairo], autentico [owtenteeko]
get (obtain) procurare [prokoorareh],
    provvedere [prov'vedaireh]
get out (of a bus, etc.) scendere [shendaireh] **>** 32, 34
get up alzarsi [alt-sarsee]
gift (present) regalo [regalo]
girl, girlfriend ragazza [ragat'sa]
give dare [dareh]; (as a gift) regalare [regalareh]
give up: to give up rinunciare [reenoonchareh],
    darsi per vinto [darsee pair veento]
gladly! (with pleasure!) volentieri [volent-yairee]
glass (for drinking) bicchiere m [beek'kyair-eh];
    (material) vetro [vetro]
glasses (spectacles) occhiali m, pl [ok'kyalee] **>** 65
go andare [andareh]
goal (aim) scopo [skopo]
God Dio [dee-yo]
good buono [bwono]
goodbye: to say goodbye congedarsi [konjedarsee],
    accomiatarsi [ak'kom-yatarsee]
government governo [govairno]
grandeur grandezza [grandet'sa]
grandfather, grandmother nonno [non'no],
    nonna [non'na]
grandson, granddaughter nipote m/f [neepoteh]
gratuity (Br: tip) mancia [mancha] **>** 35, 40
grave (tomb) tomba [tomba]
green verde [vairdeh]
greet salutare [salootareh]
grey grigio [greejo]
ground (earth) suolo [swolo]
ground floor (Am: first floor) pianoterra
    [pyanotair'ra], pianterreno [pyantair'reno]
group gruppo [groop'po]
guarantee garanzia [garant-see-ya]
guess v indovinare [eendoveenareh]
guest ospite m [ospeeteh]
guesthouse trattoria [trat'toree-ya],
    la pensione [la pen-syoneh] **>** 8, 68
guide (book) guida m [gweeda] **>** 67
guided tour visita guidata [veezeeta gweedata] **>** 79
guilt colpa [kolpa]
guitar chitarra [keetar'ra]

H

hair i capelli m, pl [ee kapel'lee] **>** 61
hairdresser's il parrucchiere
    [eel par'rook'kyair-eh] **>** 56, 61
half mezzo [met'so]
hall sala [sala], padiglione m [padeel-yoneh]
handwriting calligrafia [kal'leegrafee-ya]
happen accadere [ak'kadaireh], succedere
    [soot'chedaireh]
happy contento [kontento], felice [feleecheh];
    (fortunate) fortunato [fortoonato]

hard (solid) duro [dooro]; (difficult) difficile
    [deef'feecheeleh], duro [dooro]
hardly appena [ap'pena]
harmful dannoso [dan'noso]
have avere [avaireh]
have to dovere [dovaireh]
he lui [loo-ee]
health n salute f [salooteh]; **healthy** adv sano [sano]
hear v udire [oodeereh]
heating riscaldamento [reeskaldamento] **>** 70
heaven paradiso [paradeezo]
heavy pesante [pesanteh]
Hello! ciao [chow]; (on the phone) pronto [pronto]
help n aiuto [a-yooto]; v aiutare [a-yootareh]
her la sua [la soo-a]
here qui [kwee]
high alto [alto]
hike v camminare [kam'meenareh] **>** 87, 88
hill collina [kol'leena]
hire affittare [af'feet'tareh] **>** 76, 77
his (il) suo [(eel) soo-o]
history storia [stor-ya]
hold v tenere [tenaireh]
hole buco [booko]
holiday home casa per le vacanze
    [kasa pair leh vakant-seh] **>** 9, 74
holiday (Am: vacation) ferie f, pl [fair-yeh]
holy santo [santo], solenne [solen'neh]
home-made fatto in casa [fat'to een kasa]
hope v sperare [spairareh]
hospital l'ospedale m [lospedaleh] **>** 108
host/hostess ospite m/f [ospeeteh], padrone m/
    padrona f di casa [padroneh/padrona dee kasa]
hot caldo [kaldo]
hotel hotel m [otel] **>** 6, 68
hour ora [ora]
house casa [kasa]
household goods articoli m, pl casalinghi
    [arteekolee kasaleen-gee]
how long? per quanto tempo? [pair kwanto tempo]
how many? quanti/quante? [kwantee/kwanteh]
how much? quanto/quanta? [kwanto/kwanta]
how? come? [komeh]
however però [pairo], tuttavia [toot'tavee-ya]
hug v abbracciare [ab'brat'chareh]
hunger n fame f [fameh]
hungry affamato [af'famato]
hurt v far male [far maleh]
husband marito [mareeto]

I

I io [ee-yo]
idea idea [eed-ay-a]
identity card (ID) tessera [tes'saira],
    carta d'identità [karta deedenteeta]
if se [seh]

ill (Am: sick)   malato [malato] **>** 110
illness   malattia [malat'tee-ya] **>** 110
immediately   subito [soobeeto]
impolite   scortese [skorteseh]
import n   importazione f [eemportat-syoneh]
important   importante [eemportanteh]
impossible   impossibile [eempos'seebeeleh]
in   in [een]
in addition   inoltre [eenoltreh], oltre a [oltreh a]
included (in the price, etc.)   compreso [kompreso]
inform   informare qlc [eenformareh (kwalkoono)],
   comunicare [komooneekareh]
information   informazione f [eenformat-syoneh]
information office/bureau   ufficio informazioni
   [oof'feechyo eenformat-syonee]
   > 20, 23, 29, 31, 32, 78
inhabitant   abitante m/f [abeetanteh]
innocent   innocente [een'nochenteh]
insect   insetto [eenset'to]
inside   dentro [dentro]
inspect (check)   seguire con lo sguardo [segweereh
   kon lo zgwardo], verificare [vaireefeekareh],
   controllare [kontrol'lareh]
instead of   invece di [eenvecheh dee]
insult v   offendere [of'fendaireh]
insurance   assicurazione f [as'seekoorat-syoneh]
interested: to be interested (in)   interessarsi (di)
   [eentaires'sarsee dee]
international   internazionale [eentairnat-syonaleh]
Internet   internet f [eentairnet]
interrupt   interrompere [eentair'rompaireh];
   interruption l'interruzione f [leentair'root-syoneh]
introduction (person)   presentazione f
   [prezentat-syoneh]
invalid (void)   invalido [eenvaleedo]
invite v   invitare [eenveetareh]
invoice amount (billing amount)   importo [eemporto]
Ireland, Eire   Irlanda [eerlanda]
island   isola [eezola]
isn't it?   non è vero? [non eh vairo]
Italian (language) italiano [eetal-yano]; (Italian man/
   woman) italiano/italiana [eetal-yano/eetal-yana]
Italy   Italia [eetal-ya]

jellyfish   medusa [medooza]
jewellery   gioiello [joyel'lo] **>** 65
job (position)   posto [posto]
joke   scherzo [skairt-so]
journey   viaggio [vee-yaj'jo]; (return journey) ritorno
   in patria [reetorno een patree-ya], rientro [ree-yentro]
joy   gioia [joya]
judge v   giudicare [joodeekareh]
just (a moment ago)   proprio ora [propree-yo ora]
just as... (good) as   tanto ... (bene) quanto
   [tanto ... (beneh) kwanto]

keep v   tenere [tenaireh]
key n   la chiave [la kyaveh] **>** 70, 74
kind adj   caro [karo], gentile [jenteeleh], amabile
   [amabeeleh]; (kindness) gentilezza [jenteelet'sa],
   cortesia [kortezee-ya]
kiss   n bacio [bachyo]; v baciare [bachareh]
kitchen   cucina [koocheena]
knife   coltello [koltel'lo]
know   conoscere [konoshaireh]; (get to know s.o.)
   conoscere qlc [konoshaireh kwalkoono], fare la
   conoscenza di qlc [fareh la konoshent-sa dee
   kwalkoono] **>** 11

lack   difetto [deefet'to]
ladder   scala [skala]
lady   signora [seen-yora]
lake   lago [lago]
land (ground)   terra [tair'ra]
landlord/lady   il padrone/la padrona (di casa)
   [eel padroneh/la padrona (dee kasa)] **>** 74;
   oste m [osteh]/ostessa f [ostes'sa]
landscape   paesaggio [pa-yezaj'jo]
language   lingua [leen-gwa]
last   v durare [doorareh];
   adj ultimo/ultima [oolteemo/oolteema]
late   tardi [tardee]; (to be late) ritardare [reetardareh]
later   più tardi [pyoo tardee]
laugh v   ridere [reedaireh]
lawn   prato (rasato) [prato (rasato)]
lazy   pigro [peegro]
learn   imparare [eemparareh]
leave (for)   partire (per) [parteereh (pair)];
   (hit the road) mettersi in cammino
   [met'tairsee een kam'meeno]
left: on the left   a sinistra [a seeneestra]
lend   prestare [prestareh]
length (measure, distance)   lunghezza [loon-get'sa],
   distanza [deestant-sa]
less   (di) meno [(dee) meno]
let (allow)   lasciare [lash-yareh]
letter (mail)   lettera [let'taira] **>** 114
lie down   sdraiarsi [zdra-yarsee]
lie n (untruth)   bugia [booja]
life   vita [veeta]
lifeboat   scialuppa di salvataggio
   [sh-yaloop'pa dee salvataj'jo] **>** 33
lift (Am: elevator)   ascensore m [ashensoreh]
light adj   (bright) chiaro [kyaro];
   (weight) luce f [loocheh]
light n   luce f [loocheh]
lightning   fulmine m [foolmeeneh], flash m [flash]
like   v piacere [pya-chaireh]; (comparison) come
   [komeh]; (like that) così [kosee]

line (Br: queue) fila [feela]

listen ascoltare [askoltareh]

little piccolo [peek'kolo]

little: a little bit of... un po' di ... [oon po dee]

live v vivere [veevaireh]; (reside) abitare [abeetareh]

located: to be located trovarsi [trovarsee]

location posizione f [pozeet-syoneh]

lock n serratura [sair'ratoora]; v chiudere a chiave [kyoodaireh a kyaveh]

lodge (chalet) capanna [kapan'na]; (mountain hut) baita [ba-yeeta]

lone, lonely solo [solo], solitario [soleetar-yo]

long lungo [loon-go]

long-distance call interurbana [eentairoorbana] ➤ 116

look after (take care of) stare attento a [stareh at'tento a]

look out! attenzione! [at'tent-syoneh]

look v guardare [gwardareh]; (look for) cercare [chairkareh]

lorry il camion [eel kam-yon]

lose v perdere [pairdaireh] ➤ 113

loss n perdita [pairdeeta]

lost property office ufficio oggetti smarriti [oof'feechyo oj'jet'tee zmar'reetee] ➤ 113

lost: to get lost v smarrirsi [zmar'reer-see]

lot: a lot of molto [molto]

loud rumoroso [roomor-oso]

loudspeaker altoparlante m [altoparlanteh]

love v amare [amareh]

low basso [bas'so]

low season bassa stagione f [bas'sa stajoneh] ➤ 71

luck n felicità [feleecheeta]; **lucky** adj fortunato [fortoonato]

luggage (baggage) bagaglio [bagal-yo] ➤ 29, 32

lunch pranzo [prand-zo], il desinare [eel dezeenareh] ➤ 40

M

machine macchina [mak'keena]

made from (material) di [dee]

magazine rivista [reeveesta] ➤ 67

maiden name il nome da ragazza [eel nomeh da ragat'sa]

mail v (post) imbucare [eembookareh] ➤ 113

mainland terraferma [tair'rafairma] ➤ 33

make up one's mind decidersi [decheedairse]

make v produrre [prodoor'reh]; (make tea/coffee) fare il tè/il caffè [fareh eel teh/eel kaf'feh]

male maschile [maskeeleh]

man uomo [womo]

manager direttore m/direttrice f [deeret'toreh/deeret'treecheh]

map carta geografica [karta jayografeeka] ➤ 67; (of a town/city) pianta della città [pyanta del'la cheet'ta] ➤ 67, 78; (walking/hiking) mappa dei sentieri [map'pa day sent-yairee] ➤ 67, 88

market mercato [mairkato] ➤ 56, 81

marriage matrimonio [matree-mon-yo]

married (to) sposato (con) [spozato [kon]]

marry sposare [spozareh]

mass (relig.) messa [mes'sa]

material stoffa [stof'fa]

matter n faccenda [fat'chenda]

maybe forse [forseh]

me mi [mee], me [meh]

meal pasto [pasto]; (course, dish) pietanza [pye-tant-sa]

mean v (signify) significare [seen-yeefeekareh]

measurements le misure [leh meezooreh]

meat carne f [karneh] ➤ 44, 48, 65

medicine medicina [medeecheena], farmaco [farmako] ➤ 57, 60, 107

Mediterranean Sea Mediterraneo [medeetair'ran-ayo]

meet incontrare [eenkontrareh]; (run into, come across) trovare [trovareh]

memorise tenere a mente qc [tenaireh a menteh kwalkosa]

menu il menù [eel menoo] ➤ 38, 46

message notizia [noteet-sya]

middle mezzo [met'so], centro [chentro]

minus meno [meno]

minute n minuto [meenooto]

misfortune sfortuna [sfortoona], sventura [zventoora]

Miss (title) signorina [seen-yoreena]

miss v (a bus etc.) perdere [pairdaireh]; (someone, etc.) mancare [mankareh]

mistake sbaglio [zbal-yo], errore m [air'roreh]; (by mistake) erroneamente [air'ron-yamenteh], per sbaglio [pair zbal-yo]; (to be mistaken) sbagliarsi [zbal-yarsee]

misunderstand fraintendere [fra-eentendaireh]

mixed misto [meesto]

mobile phone (Am. cell phone) il cellulare/telefonino [eel chel'loolareh/telefoneeno] ➤ 116

modern moderno [modairno]

moment istante m [eestanteh], momento [momento]

money denaro [denaro] ➤ 104

month mese m [meseh] ➤ 18

moon n luna [loona]

more più [pyoo]

morning mattino [mat'teeno], mattina [mat'teena]; (in the morning) la mattina (presto) [la mat'teena (presto)]

mosquito zanzara [dzand-zara]

mother madre f [madreh]

motive (reason, cause) motivo [moteevo]

motor (engine) il motore [eel motoreh] ➤ 24, 27

motorbike motocicletta [motocheeklet'ta] ➤ 23

mountain monte m [monteh], montagna [montan-ya] ➤ 81

DICTIONARY

move house cambiare casa [kamb-yareh kasa]

movie film m [feelm] > 83

Mr/Mrs signor/signora [seen-yor/seen-yora]

mud fango [fan-go]

museum museo [moozayo] > 79, 81

music musica [moozeeka]

my (il) mio [(eel) mee-yo]

N

naked nudo [noodo]

name nome m [nomeh] > 11

nation nazione f [nat-syoneh]

nationality nazionalità [nat-syonaleeta]

natural adj naturale [natooraleh]

nature natura [natoora]

nausea nausea [nows-aya] > 110

near adj vicino [veecheeno];
  adv vicino a [veecheeno a]

nearby vicino [veecheeno]

necessary necessario [neches'sar-yo]

need v aver bisogno di [avair beezon-yo dee]

neighbour vicino/vicina [veecheeno/veecheena]

neither neppure [nep'pooreh]

nephew nipote m [neepoteh]

nervous nervoso [nairvoso]

never mai [ma-ee], **nevertheless** ciò nonostante [ch-yo nonostanteh], tuttavia [toot'tavee-ya]

new nuovo [nwovo]

news (news) notiziario [noteet-syar-yo]; (interesting information) novità [noveeta]

newsagent's, news stand edicola (dei giornali) [edeekola (day jornalee)]

newspaper giornale m [jornaleh] > 67

next prossimo [pros'seemo]; (next to) vicino a [veecheeno a]; (the next) prossimo [pros'seemo]

nice simpatico [seempateeko]

niece nipote f [neepoteh]

night notte f [not'teh]; (spend the night) pernottare [pairnot'tareh] > 68

night club il night-club [eel na-eet-klab] > 82

nobody nessuno [nes'soono]

noise rumore m [roomoreh], chiasso [kyas'so]

none/no nessuno [nes'soono]

noon mezzogiorno [met'sojorno]; (at noon) a mezzogiorno [a met'sojorno]

normal normale [normaleh]

north nord m [nord]

not non [non]; (not at all) in nessun caso [een nes'soon kazo]; (not even) neppure [nep'pooreh]

nothing niente [nyenteh]

now ora [ora], adesso [ades'so]

nowhere in nessun luogo [een nes'soon lwogo]

number numero [noomairo]

nun suora [swora]

nurse infermiere m [eenfairm-yaireh], infermiera f [eenfairm-yaira]

O

object n oggetto [oj'jet'to]

observe (the rules) osservare [os'sairvareh]

obtain ottenere [ot'tenaireh]

occasion occasione f [ok'kaz-yoneh]

occupied occupato [ok'koopato]

of di [dee], da [da]

of course adv naturalmente [natooralmenteh]

offend offendere [of'fendaireh]

offer v offrire [of'freereh]

office ufficio [oof'feechyo]

often spesso [spes'so]

oil olio [ol-yo]

old vecchio [vek'kyo]; (former, ancient) antico [anteeko]

on prep su [soo], sopra [sopra]

on the contrary! certo! [chairto], sì! [see]

once (one time) una volta [oona volta]

one (number) uno [oono]; (pronoun) si [see]

only solo [solo]

open adj aperto [apairto]; v aprire [apreereh]

opening hours orari m, pl d'apertura [oraree dapairtoora]

opinion opinione f [opeen-yoneh]

opportunity opportunità f [op'portooneeta] > 109

oppose sth essere contrario [es'saireh kontrar-yo]

opposite n contrario [kontrar-yo], opposto [op'posto]; (location) di fronte [dee fronteh]

optician ottico [ot'teeko] > 56, 65

or oppure [op'pooreh]

order n l'ordinazione f [lordeenat-syoneh] > 38

organs: (internal) organs (interni) organi m, pl [(eentairnee) organee]

origin provenienza [proven-yent-sa] > 14

other: the other l'altro [laltro]

our (il) nostro [(eel) nostro]

out of order fuori uso [fwore oozo]

outside/outdoors all'aperto [al'lapairto], fuori [fwore]

oven n forno [forno]

over sopra [sopra], su [soo]

overseas oltremare m [oltremareh]

overtake sorpassare [sorpas'sareh]

owe v dovere [dovaireh]

own v possedere [pos'sedaireh]

owner proprietario/a [propree-yetar-yo/-ya]

P

pack v fare le valigie [fareh leh valeej-yeh]

package (small) pacchetto [pak'ket'to]

page pagina [pajeena]

pain dolore m [doloreh], i dolori pl [ee dolore]

painting n quadro [kwadro]

pair: a pair un paio [oon pa-yo]; (a pair of) un paio di [oon pa-yo dee]

papers (official documents) i documenti [ee dokoomentee] > 27, 118

parcel pacco [pak'ko] **>** 114
Pardon? Sorry? come scusi? [komeh skoozee]
parents genitori m, pl [jeneetoree]
park parcheggiare [parkej'jareh] **>** 23; n parco [parko], giardino pubblico [jardeeno poob'bleeko]
part (piece) parte f [parteh]
pass (mountain) passo [pas'so]
passage transito [transeeto], passaggio [pas'saj'jo]
passenger passeggero [pas'sej'jairo]
passing through (in transit) di passaggio [dee pas'saj'jo]
passport passaporto [pas'saporto] **>** 22, 105
passport control controllo passaporti [kontrol'lo pas'saportee] **>** 22
past (the past) passato [pas'sato]; (go past) davanti [davantee]
path sentiero [sent-yairo]
pay duties/customs tax sdoganare [zdog-anareh]
pay in cash pagare in contanti [pagareh een kontantee]
pay v pagare [pagareh]
payment pagamento [pagamento]
peace pace f [pacheh]
people gente f [jenteh]; (the people, citizens) popolo [popolo]
per a [a], per [pair]
per cent percento [pairchento]
percentage percentuale f [pairchentoo-aleh]
performance (theatre, etc.) rappresentazione f [rap'prezentat-syoneh], spettacolo [spet'takolo] **>** 83
perhaps forse [forseh]
permission permesso [pairmes'so]
person persona [pairsona]
petrol (Am: gas) benzina [bend-zeena] **>** 23
petrol station (Am: gas station) stazione di servizio [stat-syoneh dee sairveet-syo] **>** 23, 28
pharmacy farmacia [farmacha] **>** 57, 60
phone n telefono [telefono] **>** 114; v telefonare [telefonareh] **>** 114
phone call telefonata [telefonata] **>** 115
photo foto f [foto], fotografia [fotografee-ya]
photo: take a photo fotografare [fotografareh] **>** 113
photographic equipment gli articoli fotografici [l-yee arteekolee fotografeechee] **>** 56, 59
piece pezzo [pet'so]
pillow cuscino [koosheeno]
pity: it's a pity è un peccato [eh oon pek'kato]
place (location) luogo [lwogo], posto [posto]
plain (geog.) pianura [pyanoora]
plant n pianta [pyanta]
play v (a game) giocare [jokareh]; (an instrument) suonare [swonareh]
please per favore [pair favoreh] **>** 12; (don't mention it) prego [prego]
pleased (happy) lieto [lyeto]; (satisfied) contento [kontento], soddisfatto [sod'deesfat'to];

(to be pleased) essere contento [es'saireh kontento]; (pleased to meet you!) piacere [pya-chaireh]
pleasure n piacere m [pya-chaireh]
plus più [pyoo]
poison veleno [veleno]
poisoning avvelenamento [av'velenamento] **>** 111
police polizia [poleet-see-ya] **>** 117
polite cortese [kortezeh]
politics politica [poleeteeka]
poor (not rich) povero [povairo]
port (harbour) porto [porto] **>** 32
position posizione f [pozeet-syoneh]
possible possibile [pos'seebeeleh]
post office ufficio postale [oof'feechyo postaleh] **>** 56, 113
post v (mail) imbucare [eembookareh] **>** 113
postpone rimandare [reemandareh]
pot (for cooking) pentola [pentola]
pottery ceramiche f, pl [chairameekeh], ceramica [chairameeka]
prayer preghiera [preg-yaira]
prefer preferire [prefaireereh]
pregnant incinta [eencheenta], gravida [graveeda]
prescribe prescrivere [preskreevaireh] **>** 108
present (gift) regalo [regalo]
present: to be present essere presente [es'saireh prezenteh]
pretty adj grazioso [grat-syoso], bellino [bel'leeno]
price prezzo [pret'so]
priest prete m [preteh]
prison la prigione [la preejoneh] **>** 118
prize premio [prem-yo]
probable adj probabile [probabeeleh]; probably adv probabilmente [probabeelmenteh]
profession professione f [profes'syoneh]
programme n (Am: program) programma m [program'ma] **>** 83
promise n promessa [promes'sa]; v promettere [promet'taireh]
pronounce pronunciare [pronoonchareh]
protection protezione f [protet-syoneh]
public pubblico [poob'bleeko]
public holiday giorno festivo [jorno festeevo] **>** 18
public transport trasporti m, pl pubblici [trasportee poob'bleechee] **>** 34
pull v tirare [teerareh]
punishment pena [pena]
purse portamonete m [portamoneteh]
push v spingere [speenjaireh]
put mettere [met'taireh]

Q

quality n qualità [kwaleeta]
question n domanda [domanda]; (problem) questione f [kwest-yoneh], problema m [problema]

DICTIONARY

queue (Am: line)   fila [feela]
quick adj   svelto [zvelto], rapido [rapeedo], veloce [velocheh]; **quickly** adv   rapidamente [rapeedamenteh], presto [presto], velocemente [velochementeh]
quiet adj   tranquillo [trankweel'lo], silenzioso [seelent-syoso]; **quietly** adv   piano [pyano], silenziosamente [seelent-syo-samenteh]
quite   abbastanza [ab'bastant-sa]

R

radio   radio f [rad-yo]
railway line   linea [leen-aya]
railway/railroad   ferrovia [fair'rovee-ya] **➤ 31**
rain v   piovere [pyo-vaireh]
ramp   rampa [rampa]
rape n   violenza (carnale) [vee-yolent-sa (karnaleh)], stupro [stoopro] **➤ 117**
rare adj   raro [raro];
  rarely adv   raramente [raramenteh]
rather   piuttosto [pyoot'tosto]
reach v   raggiungere [raj'joon-jaireh]
read v   leggere [lej'jaireh]
ready   pronto [pronto]
realize   accorgersi [ak'korjairsee], rendersi conto [rendairsee konto]
reason   causa [kowsa]
receipt   ricevuta [reechevoota]
receipt: make a receipt   dare la ricevuta [dareh la reechevoota]
receive   ricevere [reechevaireh]
recent adj   recente [rechenteh];
  recently adv   recentemente [rechentementeh];
  (the other day) l'altro giorno [laltro jorno]
reception   (welcome) ricevimento [reecheveemento], (hotel) l'accettazione f [lat'chet'tat-syoneh], la reception [la ree-sep-shyon] **➤ 69**
recognize   riconoscere [reekonoshaireh]
recommend   raccomandare [rak'komandareh]
recover (after illness, etc.)   rimettersi [reemet'tairsee], riposarsi [reeposarsee]
red   rosso [ros'so]
reduction   riduzione f [reedoot-syoneh] **➤ 32**
refuse v   rifiutare [reef-yootareh]
region   regione f [rejoneh], luogo [lwogo]
register (baggage)   consegnare [konsen-yareh] **➤ 31**
registration   l'accettazione f [lat'chet'tat-syoneh]
related (family)   imparentato [eemparentato]
reluctantly   malvolentieri [malvolent-yairee]
remedy   medicina [medeecheena] **➤ 57, 60**
remember   ricordare [reekordareh]
remind s.o. of sth   ricordasi [reekordasee], ricordare qlc a qc [reekordareh kwalkoono a kwalkosa]
rent n   pigione f [peejoneh], affitto [af'feet'to] **➤ 74**
rental car   macchina a noleggio [mak'keena a nolej'jo] **➤ 29**

repair   v risarcire [reesarcheereh]; n riparazione f [reeparat-syoneh]
repeat v   ripetere [reepetaireh]
replace   sostituire [sosteetoo-eereh]
replacement   risarcimento [reesarcheemento]
reply v   rispondere [reespondaireh]
request n   domanda [domanda] **➤ 12**
reservation   la prenotazione [la prenotat-syoneh] **➤ 37, 72**
residence (place of)   domicilio [domee-cheel-yo], residenza [reseedent-sa] **➤ 22**
responsible   responsabile [responsabeeleh]; (in charge) competente [kompetenteh]
rest n   (a break) riposo [reeposo]; (the rest) resto [resto]
restaurant   ristorante m [reestoranteh] **➤ 36**
restless   irrequieto [eer'rekwee-yeto], agitato [ajeetato]
result   risultato [reesooltato]
return   n ritorno [reetorno]; v ritornare [reetornareh]
ribbon   nastro [nastro]
rich (money)   ricco [reek'ko]
right   (correct) corretto [kor'ret'to]; (just) giusto [joosto]; (appropriate: person, clothes, time etc.) adatto [adat'to]; (entitlement) diritto [deereet'to]
right: on the right   a destra [a destra]
right: to be right   aver ragione [avair rajoneh]
ring (doorbell, etc.)   suonare [swonareh]
risk n   rischio [reesk-yo]
river   fiume m [fyoomeh]
riverbank   sponda [sponda]
road map   carta automobilistica [karta owtomobeeleesteeka] **➤ 28**
road sign   il segnavia [eel sen-yavee-ya]
rock   roccia [rot'cha]
room   stanza [stant-sa], sala [sala]; (bedroom) camera [kamaira]
rotten   marcio [marchyo]
round adj   rotondo [rotondo]
route   itinerario [eeteenair-ar-yo]
rubbish n (Am: garbage)   immondizia [eem'mondeet-sya]
rule n   regolamento [regolamento]
run v (on foot)   correre [kor raireh]

S

sad   triste [treesteh]
sadness (sorrow)   dolore m [doloreh], dispiacere m [deesp-ya-chaireh]
safety pin   spillo di sicurezza [speel'lo dee seekooret'sa]
sale n   vendita [vendeeta]
same   adj stesso [stes'so], uguale [oog-waleh]; (the same thing) lo stesso [lo stes'so]
satisfied   contento [kontento], soddisfatto [sod'deesfat'to]

sausage salume m [saloomeh] > 44

save v (a life, etc.) salvare [salvareh]

say v dire [deereh]

Scotland Scozia [skot-sya]

Scots(man/woman) scozzese m/f [skot'se-seh]

sea mare m [mareh]

sea urchin riccio (di mare) [reet'chyo (dee mareh)]

season stagione f [stajoneh] > 18

seat sede f [sedeh], posto [posto]

second n (unit of time) secondo [sekondo]

secret adj, **secretly** adv segreto [segreto]

secret: in secret di nascosto [dee naskosto]

security sicurezza [seekooret'sa]

see v vedere [vedaireh]; (see again) rivedere [reevedaireh]

self-service shop/store il self-service [eel self-sairvees]

send v mandare [mandareh], inviare [eenvee-yareh]

sender (package, etc.) il mittente [eel meet'tenteh] > 114

sentence (phrase) frase f [frazeh]

separate adj separato [separato]

serious serio [sair-yo]

serve servire [sairveereh]

service (relig.) messa [mes'sa], la funzione sacra [la foont-syoneh sakra] > 81; (restaurant) servizio [sairveet-syo]

service/rest station (motorway/highway) la stazione di servizio [la stat-syoneh dee sairveet-syo], posto di ristoro [posto dee reestoro]

settle (a matter) sbrigare [zbree-gareh]

severe (illness, etc.) grave [graveh]

sex sesso [ses'so]

shade (colour) tono [tono], tonalità [tonaleeta]

shades (sunglasses) occhiali pl da sole [ok'kyalee da soleh]

shameless (impertinent) sfacciato [sfat'chato]

she lei [lay]

ship la nave [la naveh] > 33

shoe scarpa [skarpa] > 66

shop n (store) negozio [negot-syo] > 54; (business) affare m [af'fareh]

shop: to go shopping fare la spesa [fareh la spesa] > 54

shore sponda [sponda]

short (height) basso [bas'so]

short corto [korto]

shortage mancanza [mankant-sa]

shot n (gun, etc.) colpo [kolpo]

shout v gridare [greedareh]

show v mostrare [mostrareh]; (indicate) indicare [eendeekareh]

shut v chiudere [kyoo-daireh]

shy intimidire [eenteemeedeereh]

sick (Br. ill) malato [malato] > 110

side parte f [parteh], lato [lato]

sights (tourism) le cose da vedersi [leh koseh da vedairseh] > 79

sightseeing tour of a town/city giro della città [jeero del'la cheet'ta] > 79, 81

sign n insegna [eensen-ya], targa [targa], segnale m [sen-yaleh]

signature firma [feerma] > 106

silence n silenzio [seelent-syo]

silent: to be silent tacere [tachaireh]

silently silenzioso [seelent-syoso]

since (time) da [da]; (because) perché [pairkeh]; (since when) da quando? [da kwando]

sing cantare [kantareh]

single (relationship status) celibe m [cheleebeh], nubile f [noobeeleh] > 22

sister sorella [sorel'la]

sister-in-law cognata [kon-yata]

sit v sedere [sedaireh], sedersi [sedairseh]

situated: to be situated giacere [jachaireh]

situation situazione f [seetoo-at-syoneh]

size (body) statura [statoora]; (clothes, shoes) misura [meezoora]

sky cielo [ch-yelo]

sleep v dormire [dormeereh]

slim (thin) snello [znel'lo]

slow adj lento [lento]; **slowly** adv lentamente [lentamenteh]

small piccolo [peek'kolo]

small talk chiacchiere [kyak'kyaireh] > 14

smell n odore m [odoreh]

smell v sentire odore [senteereh odoreh]

smoke fumare [foomareh]; (non-/smoker) (non) fumatore [(non) foomatoreh]

smuggle v fare contrabbando [fareh kontrab'bando]

snack bar bar [bar]

snack n spuntino [spoon-teeno]

snow v nevicare [neveekareh]

so, thus dunque [doonkweh], allora [al'lora]

society società [soch-yeta], associazione f [as'sochat-syoneh], compagnia [kompan-yee-a]

soft morbido [morbeedo]; (sound, colour) tenue [tenoo-eh]

solid (firm) fermo [fairmo], saldo [saldo]

some alcuni [alkoonee], alcune [alkooneh]

somebody qualcuno [kwalkoono]

something qualcosa [kwalkosa]

sometimes a volte [a volteh]

son figlio [feel-yo]

song canzone f [kant-soneh]

soon presto [presto]

sort n (kind) specie f [spech-yeh]

sort out regolare [regolareh]

source (information, etc.) sorgente f [sorjenteh], fonte f [fonteh]

south sud m [sood]

souvenir souvenir [sooveneer] > 66

space   spazio [spat-syo]

speak   parlare [parlareh]

speed n   velocità [velocheeta]

spell v   sillabare [seel'labareh]

spoiled (ruined)   (food, etc.) avariato [avar-yato], guasto [gwasto]; (child) viziato [veet-syato]

spoon   cucchiaio [kook'kya-yo]

sport   sport m [sport] ➤ 84

sports field   campo sportivo [kampo sporteevo]

spring, source (water)   sorgente f [sorjenteh], fonte f [fonteh]

square (town/city, etc.)   piazza [pyat'sa] ➤ 81

staff   personale m [pairsonaleh]

stairs, staircase   scala [skala]

stamp v (e.g. a ticket)   affrancare [af'frankareh] ➤ 114

stand v   stare (in piedi) [stareh (een pye-dee)]

star   stella [stel'la]

start v   iniziare [eeneet-syareh]

state   stato [stato]

station   la stazione [la stat-syoneh] ➤ 31

stationery n   articoli m, pl di cartoleria [arteekolee dee kartolairee-ya] ➤ 67

stay n   soggiorno [soj'jorno]

stay v   rimanere [reemanaireh]

steal v   rubare [roobareh]

steep   ripido [reepeedo]

still (e.g. still more)   ancora [ankora]

sting v   pungere [poonjaireh]

stone   pietra [pyetra]

stop (bus stop, etc.)   fermata [fairmata] ➤ 35

stop v   fermare [fairmareh], fermarsi [fairmarsee]; (give up) smettere [zmet'taireh]

stop!   alt! [alt]

stopover/layover   fermata [fairmata] ➤ 30

store (Br: shop)   negozio [negot-syo] ➤ 54; (business) affare m [af'fareh]

storm n   temporale m [temporaleh]

story (tale)   storia [stor-ya]

stove n   stufa [stoofa]

straight on   diritto [deereet'to]

stranger   forestiero/forestiera [forest-yairo/forest-yaira]

street (road)   via [vee-ya], strada [strada]; (in the countryside) strada provinciale [strada proveenchaleh]

study v   studiare [stood-yareh]

stupid   stupido [stoopeedo], scemo [shemo]

style   lo stile [lo steeleh]

suburb   sobborgo [sob'borgo]

subway   sottopassaggio [sot'to-pas'saj'jo]

success   successo [soot'ches'so], riuscita [ree-oosheeta]

sudden adj   improvviso [eemprov'veezo]; **suddenly** adv   improvvisamente [eemprov'veezamenteh]

suitcase   valigia [valeeja]

sum (math.)   somma [som'ma]

summit   (mountain) cima [cheema], vetta [vet'ta], sommità [som'meeta]; (fig.) culmine m [koolmeeneh]; (politics) summit m [soom'meet]

sun n   sole m [soleh]; **sunny** adj   soleggiato [solej'jato], assolato [as'solato]

sunglasses (shades)   occhiali m, pl da sole [ok'kyalee da soleh]

supermarket   supermercato [soopairmairkato] ➤ 56

supplement n   supplemento [soop'plemento] ➤ 32

sure adj   sicuro [seekooro]; **surely** adv   certamente [chairtamenteh]

surname   il cognome [eel kon-yomeh] ➤ 22

surprised   sorpreso [sorpreso]

swear v   imprecare [eemprekareh]

sweat v   sudare [soodareh]

swim v   nuotare [nwotareh] ➤ 84

swimming pool   piscina [peesheena]

switch (light, etc.)   interruttore m [eentair'root'toreh]

sympathy (condolences)   condoglianze pl [kondol-yant-seh]

T

table   tavolo [tavolo], tavola [tavola]

take part (in)   prendere parte (a) [prendaireh parteh (a)]

take place   aver luogo [avair lwogo]

take v   prendere [prendaireh]; (remove, steal) portar via [portar vee-ya]; (the bus, etc.) prendere [prendaireh]; (bring, carry) portare [portareh]; (take someone somewhere) portare [portareh]

take-off   decollo [dekol'lo] ➤ 29

talk v   discorrere [deeskor'raireh], parlare [parlareh]

tall   alto [alto]

taste   n gusto [goosto], sapore m [saporeh]; v assaggiare [as'saj'jareh]

tax   tassa [tas'sa], imposta [eemposta]

taxi   tassi m [tas'see] ➤ 35

telephone line   comunicazione f [komooneekat-syoneh]

telephone n   telefono [telefono] ➤ 116

tell v   raccontare [rak'kontareh]

temperature   temperatura [tempairatoora] ➤ 19

terrible   spaventoso [spaventoso], terribile [tair'reebeeleh]

than (comparison)   di [dee], che [keh]

thank (s.o.)   ringraziare qc [reen-grat-syareh kwalkoono] ➤ 12

thanks   grazie [grat-syeh] ➤ 12

that's why   perciò [pairch-yo]

theatre   teatro [tay-atro] ➤ 83

theft   furto [foorto] ➤ 117

their   loro: il loro m [eel loro], la loro f [la loro]; i loro m, pl [ee loro], le loro f, pl [leh loro]

then   allora [al'lora], poi [poy]

there   là [la]; (over there) laggiù [laj'joo]

there is, there are c'è [cheh], ci sono [chee sono]

therefore perciò [pairchyo]

they loro [loro]

thin sottile [sot'teeleh]; (slim) snello [znel'lo]

thing cosa [kosa]

think pensare [pensareh]

thirsty: to be thirsty avere sete [avaireh seteh]

this/these, that/those

(this) questo m [kwesto], questa f [kwesta];
(these) queste m [kwesteh], questi f [kwestee];
(that) quello m [kwel'lo], quella f [kwel'la];
(those) quegli m [kwel-yee], quelle f [kwel'leh]

thought n pensiero [pensyairo]

through prep per [pair], attraverso [at'travairso];
(by means of) per [pair]

ticket biglietto [beel-yet'to] ➤ 34, 35

ticket office biglietteria [beel-yet'tairee-ya]

time n tempo [tempo] ➤ 16; (time of day) l'ora
[lora] ➤ 16; (instance) volta [volta]

time: in time a tempo [a tempo], in tempo
[een tempo]

time: on time adj puntuale [poontoo-aleh];
adv puntualmente [poontoo-almenteh]

timetable orario [orar-yo] ➤ 32

tip (Am: gratuity) mancia [mancha] ➤ 35, 40

tired stanco [stanko]

tiring faticoso [fateekoso]

to a [a]

to (London) a (Londra) [a (londra)]

tobacco tabacco [tabak'ko]

today oggi [oj'jee]

together insieme [een-syemeh]

toilet toilette f [toy-let'teh], gabinetto [gabeenet'to]
➤ 37, 70, 72, 118

toilet paper carta igienica [karta eejeneeka]

tolerate, put up with sopportare [sop'portareh]

tomorrow mattino [mat'teeno], mattina [mat'teena]

tone (sound) tono [tono]

too much/many troppo [trop'po]

topic (of a conversation, etc.) argomento [argomento]

tour guide n guida [gweeda], cicerone m
[cheechaironeh]

tour n visita [veezeeta] ➤ 78

tourist information office ente m per il turismo
[enteh pair eel tooreezmo]

tow (away) rimorchiare [reemork-yareh],
trainare [traeenareh] ➤ 24

towards (direction) verso [vairso]

town città [cheet'ta]

town centre centro [chentro], centro città [chentro
cheet'ta]

town hall (Am: city hall) municipio
[mooneecheep-yo] ➤ 81

toy n giocattolo [jokat'tolo]

traffic traffico [traf'feeko]

train n treno [treno] ➤ 31

transfer v (money) rimettere [reemet'taireh],
inviare [eenvee-yareh]

transit visa permesso di transito
[pairmes'so dee transeeto]

translate tradurre [tradoor'reh]

travel agency agenzia di viaggi
[ajent-see-ya dee vee-yaj'jee]

travel v viaggiare [vee-yaj'jareh]

traveller's cheque/check assegno turistico
[as'sen-yo tooreesteeko], il traveller's chèque
[eel trav-lairzshek] ➤ 105

tree albero [albairo]

trip n gita [jeeta] ➤ 81

truck il camion [eel kam-yon]

true vero [vairo]

try v tentare [tentareh]

tunnel tunnel m [toon'nel],
galleria [gal'lairee-ya]

typical (of) tipico (di) [teepeeko (dee)]

■■■ U

ugly brutto [broot'to]

umbrella ombrello [ombrel'lo]

uncertain incerto [eenchairto], dubbio [doob'byo]

uncle zio [tsee-yo]

unconscious svenuto [zvenooto], senza
conoscenza [sent-sa konoshent-sa] ➤ 112

under sotto [sot'to]

underground (railway) metropolitana
[metropoleetana] ➤ 34

understand capire [kapeereh]

underway (in transit) per la strada [pair la strada]

uneasy inquieto [eenkwee-yeto]

unfortunately purtroppo [poortrop'po]

unfriendly sgarbato [zgarbato]

unhappy infelice [eenfeleecheh],
sfortunato [sfortoonato]

unhealthy dannoso [dan'noso], malsano [malsano]

United States Stati m, pl Uniti d'America
[statee ooneetee damaireeka]

unknown sconosciuto [skonosh-yooto]

unlucky (person) sfortunato [sfortoonato],
sventurato [zventoorato];
(event) disgraziato [deesgrat-syato]

until fino a [feeno a]

up prep sopra [sopra], sù [soo]

urgent urgente [oorjenteh];
(hurried) frettoloso [fret'toloso]

us noi [noy]; (to us) a noi [a noy]

use v usare [oozareh]

■■■ V

vacant (bathroom, etc.) libero [leebairo]

vacation vacanza [vakant-sa], ferie pl [fair-yeh]

vain: in vain invano [eenvano]

valid valido [valeedo] ➤ 22

value n valore m [valoreh]

vegetables verdura [vairdoora] ➤ 41, 49, 65

versus contro [kontro]

very molto [molto]

view n vista [veesta]

village villaggio [veel'laj'jo], località [lokaleeta]

visa visto [veesto]

visible visibile [veezee-beeleh]

visit s.o. far visita a qlc [far veezeeta a kwalkoono]

visit for visitare [veezeetareh]

voice voce f [vocheh]

volume (book) volume m [voloomeh]

vote v votare [votareh]

■ W ■

wage (salary) compenso [kompenso], premio [prem-yo], retribuzione f [retreeboot-syoneh]

wait for aspettare [aspet'tareh]

waiter/waitress il cameriere [eel kamairee-yaireh], la cameriera [la kamairee-yaira]

waiting room sala d'aspetto [sala daspet'to]

wake v svegliare [zvel-yareh]

Wales Galles m [gal'les]

walk v camminare [kam'meenareh]

walk: to go for a walk passeggiare [pas'sej'jareh]

wallet portafoglio [portafol-yo] ➤ 117

want v volere [volaireh]

war guerra [gwair'ra]

warm adj caldo [kaldo]

warn v avvertire [av'vairteereh]

warning! attenzione! [at'tent-syoneh]

wash v lavare [lavareh]

watch n orologio da polso [orolojo da polso]; v guardare [gwardareh]

water acqua [ak'kwa]; (drinking water) acqua potabile [ak'kwa potabeeleh]

way (of doing something) modo [modo], maniera [man-yaira]; (route) via [vee-ya]

we noi [noy]

weak debole [deboleh]

wear v indossare [eendos'sareh]

weather tempo [tempo] ➤ 19

web address sito internet [seeto eentairnet] ➤ 8

wedding nozze f, pl [not'seh]

week settimana [set'teemana] ➤ 18

weigh v pesare [pesareh]

weight peso [peso]

welcome! benvenuto! [benvenooto]

well adv bene [beneh]; (interjection) bene [beneh]

Welsh(man, woman) gallese [gal'leseh]

west Occidente m [ot'cheedenteh]

wet bagnato [ban-yato]; (soaking wet) fradicio [fradeechyo]; (damp, humid) umido [oomeedo]

what cosa [kosa], che cosa [keh kosa]; (what for?) a che cosa? [a keh kosa]

wheelchair carrozzella [kar'rot'sel'la], sedia a rotelle [sed-ya a rotel'leh]

when quando [kwando]

where dove [doveh]; (where from) da/di dove? [da/dee doveh]; (where to) dove? [doveh]

whether se [seh]

which? quale? sing/quali? pl [kwaleh/kwalee]

while mentre [mentreh]

white bianco [byanko]

who?, to whom? chi? [kee]

whose? di chi? [dee kee]

why? perché? [pairkeh]

wide largo [largo], ampio [amp-yo]

wife moglie f [mol-yeh]

win v vincere [veenchaireh], guadagnare [gwadan-yareh]

wish v volere [volaireh], desiderare [deseedairareh]

with con [kon]

within (time) entro [entro]

without senza [sent-sa]

witness n testimone m [testeemoneh]

woman donna [don'na]

wood (timber) legno [len-yo], legna [len-ya]

word parola [parola]

work v lavorare [lavorareh]; (function) funzionare [foont-syonareh]

working days nei giorni m, pl feriali [nay jornee fair-yalee]

workshop officina [of'feecheena] ➤ 24, 27

world mondo [mondo]

worry n (concern) problema [problema], preoccupazione f [prayok'koopat-syoneh]

worry: to worry about preoccuparsi di [prayok'kooparsee dee]

worth: to be worth a lot avere un grande valore [avaireh oon grandeh valoreh]

write scrivere [skreevaireh]

writing: in writing per iscritto [pair eeskreet'to]

wrong: to be wrong sbagliarsi [zbal-yarsee]

wrong/false sbagliato [zbal-yato]; (fraudulent/deceiving) falso [falso]

■ Y ■

year anno [an'no]

yellow giallo [jal'lo]

you pl, inf/formal inf/pl voi [voy]; formal Voi [voy]; (to you) a voi/a Voi [a voy/a voy]

you sing, inf. tu [too]; (to you) ti [tee],

young giovane [jovaneh]

your pl, formal (il) vostro [eel) vostro]

your sing, inf (il) tuo [eel) too-o]

youth hostel ostello per la gioventù [ostel'lo pair la joventoo]

>DOS & DON'TS

You're Hot and You're Cold

When it's 32 degrees in the shade and you're gasping for an ice cold glass of water, take care how you order if you don't want a shock! Asking for an *acqua calda* [akwa kalda] will send the waiter back with a glass of water... but don't get a shock – it'll be piping hot. Don't be fooled by how it looks: *caldo* [kaldo] doesn't mean cold. On a boiling hot day, you'll need to order an *acqua fredda* [akwa fred'da] ("cold water"), instead.

A Room with a View(finder)

If your camera should do the unthinkable and give up the ghost on holiday, don't ask where you can get a *camera* [kamaira] ...if you do, you'll probably be sent to the nearest hotel. *Camera* means "bedroom" in Italian – the word you're looking for if you want to keep on taking your holiday snaps is *una macchina fotografia* [oona mak'keena fotografee-ya].

It's Not Worth its Salt

If you try and order a tasty salad to go with your *spaghetti* [spaget'tee], choose your words carefully: if you say the word *salata* [salata], you might have to order a glass of water to boot: *salata* means salty. Make sure to say *insalata* [eensalata] if you're looking for a refreshingly leafy side order to accompany your meal.

Double or Nothing!

Italian words are littered with double letters. They're there for a reason: you

really need to stress them as you talk. If you don't, the effects won't be too drastic most of the time – but once in a while you'll get much more than you bargained for. If you're trying to say "year" (*anno* [an'no]), for instance, and don't stress the double 'n', you'll inadvertently say *ano* [ano] ("anus"). The same goes with a delicious variety of pasta, *penne* [pen'neh], and another similar word: *pene* [peneh] ("penis"). Be careful.

A Cat's Tail?

Cat lovers will be very happy to know that the Italian peninsula is home to a wide variety of our feline friends. If you make an unfortunate guess at the word and tell someone about a wonderful *cazzo* [kat'so] you've seen on your travels, however, you might give them the wrong impression: *cazzo* is a very rude word for a uniquely male part of the body. You'll be much safer waxing lyrical about a cute *gatto* [gat'to] you encountered on your trip round town.

Foody Faux Pas

There are some cardinal sins we foreigners commit with Italian food that would make a native weep. Here are a few pointers to avoid an international incident: never put cheese on a fish dish, never put ketchup on your pasta, never order a *cappucino* after 11am, never ask for pasta as a side dish, and don't eat anything more substantial than *gelato* [jelato] when walking along the street. Consider yourselves warned.